Learning Objectives For:

SURVIVING INFORMATION OVERLOAD

The objectives for *Surviving Information Overload* are listed below. They have been developed to guide the user to the core issues covered in this book.

THE OBJECTIVES OF THIS BOOK ARE TO HELP THE USER:

1) Discover the ways that too much information is affecting how people live and work

2) Explore multitasking and ways to use it effectively

3) Distinguish between information and knowledge

4) Learn strategies for managing information in all of its forms

5) Obtain guidelines for choosing appropriate technologies for specific needs

ASSESSING PROGRESS

NETg has developed a Crisp Series **assessment** that covers the fundamental information presented in this book. A 25-item, multiple-choice and true/false questionnaire allows the reader to evaluate his or her comprehension of the subject matter. To download the assessment and answer key, go to www.courseilt.com and search on the book title, or call 1-800-442-7477.

Assessments should not be used in any employee selection process.

About the Author

Odette Pollar is a nationally acclaimed business consultant who delivers her WorkSmart philosophy through consulting, training, speaking, and writing. Smart Ways to Work is the name of her consulting firm, the title of her syndicated column, and the theme in each of the four previous books she has authored. Her most recent title is *Take Back Your Life: Smart Ways to Simplify Daily Living*.

Odette's down-to-earth approach and nuts-and-bolts remedies provide people immediate relief from the tyrannies of technology, the glut of information, and the seemingly over-whelming demands of complex work environments. Her 20+ years of expertise in organizational development, training, and facilitation techniques have led to long-term relationships with clients such as McDonald's, VISA, Shell Oil, and Merrill Lynch.

In demand as a speaker and trainer, Odette delivers programs on personal productivity, work and life balance, diversity management, and work simplification. She has developed a series of multimedia resources, including video, audio, and CD-ROM programs.

Odette is ready to help you gain mastery over your work. She may be reached at:

Smart Ways to Work
1441 Franklin St., Suite 301
Oakland, CA 94612
Phone: 510-763-8482
Fax: 510-763-0790
E-mail: odette@smartwaystowork.com

How to Use This Book

This *Fifty-Minute™ Series Book* is a unique, user-friendly product. As you read through the material, you will quickly experience the interactive nature of the book. There are numerous exercises, real-world case studies, and examples that invite your opinion, as well as checklists, tips, and concise summaries that reinforce your understanding of the concepts presented.

A Crisp Learning *Fifty-Minute™ Book* can be used in a variety of ways. Individual self-study is one of the most common. However, many organizations use *Fifty-Minute* books for pre-study before a classroom training session. Other organizations use the books as a part of a systemwide learning program—supported by video and other media based on the content in the books. Still others work with Crisp Learning to customize the material to meet their specific needs and reflect their culture. Regardless of how it is used, we hope you will join the more than 20 million satisfied learners worldwide who have completed a *Fifty-Minute Book*.

Surviving Information Overload

How to Find, Filter, and Focus on What's Important

Odette Pollar

A Crisp Fifty-Minute™ Series Book

This Fifty-Minute™ book is designed to be "read with a pencil." It is an excellent workbook for self-study as well as classroom learning. All material is copyright-protected and cannot be duplicated without permission from the publisher. *Therefore, be sure to order a copy for every training participant by contacting:*

THOMSON

NETg

1-800-442-7477 • 25 Thomson Place, Boston MA • www.courseilt.com

Surviving Information Overload

How to Find, Filter, and Focus on What's Important

Odette Pollar

CREDITS:
Product Manager: **Debbie Woodbury**
Editor: **Ann Gosch**
roduction Editor: **Genevieve McDermott**
Production Artists: **Nicole Phillips, Rich Lehl, and Betty Hopkins**
Manufacturing: **Stephanie Porreca**

For more information contact:

> NETg
> 25 Thomson Place
> Boston, MA 02210

Or find us on the Web at **www.courseilt.com**

For permission to use material from this text or product, submit a request online at www.thomsonrights.com.

Trademarks
Crisp Fifty-Minute Series is a trademark of NETg. Some of the product names and company names used in this book have been used for identification purposes only, and may be trademarks or registered trademarks of their respective manufacturers and sellers.

Disclaimer
NETg reserves the right to revise this publication and make changes from time to time in its content without notice.

ISBN 10: 1-56052-694-7
ISBN 13: 978-1-56052-694-0
Library of Congress Catalog Card Number 2003108299
Printed in the United States

2 3 4 5 08 07 06

Foreword

Before the World Wide Web, e-mail, faxes, cell phones—and even before personal computers, when photocopy machines were young—I went to graduate school to be a librarian, a Master of Library and Information Science. How naïve and arrogant that sounds now. Although I never worked in that profession, I now use the "information management" skills I learned then every day.

One of the most important things I learned about managing information was that knowing what you want and why you want it (i.e., what you will do with it) is far more useful than knowing everything. This remains true for us today, as we face the mountainous maze of information before us—veritable libraries of news, mail, reports, memos, messages, books, articles—all in multiple formats!

So you thought we were kidding—read another book to better manage information overload?! Why should you do it? Will this be worth it? I believe so, because what this is really about is the *value* of *time*—how you use it and what you get in return. We all want to know how we can get through that maze of stuff—data, information, junk, and gems—without wasting time and with something of value to show for the time we invest.

Your guide through this maze is Odette Pollar, consultant, trainer, author, speaker, and productivity-improvement specialist. Drawing on the latest research in the field, and her own formidable knowledge, she shares powerful truths and leads you through exercises designed to help you get the most for the time you spend sifting through, searching for, managing, and using information, in whatever form it comes to you.

The truths Odette tells are these—that most of us are confused and overloaded, that you often have to go slow to go fast, that some of those "timesaving" information tools don't really save you time, that you have to *stop* and think about what's really important for you to make the best decisions, and that multi-tasking really doesn't work. (But you knew this all along!) The time you invest in the book's exercises does "slow you down," but just enough to think about what you're actually doing, what you want to be doing, and about how to bridge the inevitable gap. Odette can help you find your own truth, the information that will be useful and important to you in your work and life.

So block your calendar, forward your phone (see, you're learning already!), take a few deep breaths, and get started *Surviving Information Overload*.

Helen Argyres, MA, MLS
Manager of Employee Development
East Bay Municipal Utility District
Oakland, California

Contents

Part 4: Managing Messaging Systems

Part 5: Processing Paper

Part 6: Taming Technology

Part 7: Coping at Home

Summary

Introduction

If someone asked you to write a job description, would you include "information manager" as one of your roles? You should, because today everyone, whether you realize it or not, is an information manager.

Usually this is not a job for which you received training—or were given a raise or even acknowledgment. It is probably a job that increasingly occupies your time and attention as the amount of information you must process daily continues to grow. And no doubt the primary result of trying to handle this *information overload* is an ever-increasing level of stress, anxiety, and fatigue.

People everywhere are talking about their inability to keep up with the information that bombards them at work, at home, on vacation, out on the town, even while sitting on their sofas trying to relax. So widespread is this malady—commonly referred to as *information anxiety*—that companies, government agencies, universities, and organizations all over the country are conducting research to determine:

> ➤ **How well people are coping (not very)**

> ➤ **What is working (taking control and setting limits)**

> ➤ **What is not working (multi-tasking)**

The important point to focus on is what *is* working—taking control and setting limits. But how do you take control over information when you are being inundated by:

> ➤ **E-mail**

> ➤ **Phone calls and voice mail**

> ➤ **Piles of paper (newspapers, memos, magazines, faxes, journals, Web content)**

> ➤ **Technology that changes before you have learned the last version**

You will find the answers within the pages of *Surviving Information Overload*. The purpose of this book is to give you the training you need to succeed in your role (official or not) as information manager. As you read this book and do the exercises, you will be developing four important skills essential to this effort:

> ➤ **Focus**

> ➤ **Evaluation**

> ➤ **Decision-making**

> ➤ **Implementation**

You will learn (1) to focus on how different types of information are affecting you personally and professionally, (2) how to evaluate the options for change, (3) how to decide what will work best for you, and (4) how to implement your choices.

My goal is to help you learn to make the best use of—even enjoy—the many advantages of this Information Age.

Whether you work in a large corporate environment or out of a closet-sized home office, whether you are a student or a stay-at-home parent, or some combination of these, you will find the exercises, checklists, and examples in this book to be eye-opening and, ideally, life-changing.

You can make information work for you, rather than against you.

Odette Pollar

P A R T 1

Information Anxiety

2

Do You Have Information Anxiety?

Are you feeling overwhelmed by the sheer weight of information you are expected (or think you are expected) to deal with every day—paper, electronic data, e-mail and voice mail messages, video? Do you regularly mutter to yourself:

➤ What am I supposed to do with all this information?

➤ When will I have the time to read all this?

➤ With hundreds of Web sites popping up daily, how can I stay current?

➤ How do I determine whether the information I find on the Web is accurate?

If so, you are probably suffering from information anxiety, a form of stress caused by information overload that has become so widespread it is bordering on epidemic.

What's in a Name?

You will also hear information anxiety called *technostress, information fatigue syndrome,* and even *data asphyxiation.*

According to Richard Saul Wurman, who wrote the book on the subject, information anxiety is caused by the gap between what we understand and what we think we should understand—that is, the difference between data (information) and knowledge. It is made worse by the fact that most information is controlled by someone else, meaning we have little say about its content and how or when we receive it.

Calculating the Weight of Information Overload

You did not become overloaded by information overnight. The weight was added little by little, with each new technological invention. Consider that:

➤ Fifteen years ago, there was no widespread consumer use of e-mail, cell phones, or personal digital assistants (PDAs).

➤ Thirty years ago, the Internet was a network used only by scientists, the government, and researchers. The World Wide Web had not been invented.

➤ Before the technology "revolution," most people went home after an eight- or nine-hour shift. Today companies and workers in all fields boast about 24/7 availability. Most Americans now work an average of 47 hours a week.

What is the result of all these technological "advancements"? Too much information arriving in too many different formats. How much is too much?

A single Sunday edition of *The New York Times* today contains more information than typical 19th-century citizens faced in their entire lifetime.[1]

More new information has been produced in the last 30 years than in the last 5,000.[2] The Internet alone exceeded four billion pages in early 2001 and was growing at a rate of 7.3 million new pages every day.

In 2001, approximately 1.4 trillion e-mail messages were sent from businesses in North America alone, up from 40 billion in 1995.[3]

Media watchers predict that, by 2004, there will be 18,000 magazine titles (there were 4,500 in 1960), 200 television stations (4 in 1960), 2,400 Internet radio stations (none in 1960), and 20 million Internet sites.[4]

New electronic devices have not, as promised, slowed the flow of paper. In fact, an average of 80–90% of all records in an organization are still paper-based (of which 30–40% represent duplicate–unnecessary?–copies of records that are maintained elsewhere in the organization).[5]

Food for Thought

"Better information processing can speed the flow of data, but is of little help in reading the printout, deciding what to do about it, or finding a higher meaning. Meaning requires time-consuming thought and the pace of modern life works against affording us the time to think."

–Orrin Klapp
Overload and Boredom: Essays on the Quality of Life in the Information Society

How Are You Managing Now?

How are you currently handling this onslaught of information? Probably for a while now, you have been dealing with this problem by not dealing with it—which only makes your symptoms of, or vulnerability to, information anxiety worse. Find out how you are faring by taking the following quiz. Check (✔) the box for the statements that apply to you:

❑ Do you put off answering e-mail and voice mail messages to the point that it is "getting you in trouble" with colleagues, family, and friends?

❑ Do you have stacks of out-of-date unread newspapers and magazines in your office and home? Do you promise yourself you will get to them "one of these days"? Or have you given up and just thrown out publications without reading them?

❑ Do you delete without reading the online newsletters you have signed up to receive? Or do you file them electronically or print them out, planning—hoping—one day to get to them?

❑ Are you always doing three things at once or switching between tasks so frequently that you get nothing done? Or do you have trouble remembering what you did a few hours earlier?

❑ Do you feel you never really listen to anyone anymore because your mind is always on the next thing or the last thing—or everything? Is "uh-huh" your favorite response?

❑ Do you feel like a prisoner of technology—handcuffed to your cell phone, pager, palmtop, laptop, desktop?

❑ Are you more irritable these days? Do you find yourself snapping at colleagues, friends, and family, or getting into arguments over nothing?

❑ Do you fantasize about running away?

❑ Do you go to bed feeling as though you did not get anything done, then sleep badly because you are worrying about tomorrow?

Add your own:

❑ _____

❑ _____

❑ _____

If you checked three or more boxes on the previous page, you are past the information-tolerance limit, and it is time to take action!

It's Sickening

Did you know that besides making you feel frustrated and inefficient, information anxiety could also make you physically sick? Studies conducted over a period of 30 years list many symptoms resulting from information overload: rising blood pressure and cardiovascular problems, weakened vision, repetitive stress injuries, and backaches.

Another survey reported that 1 in 4 of more than 1,300 managers said they suffered ill health as a result of the amount of information they handle.[6]

That is the bad news. The good news is, there are lots of things you can do to relieve the symptoms of information fatigue syndrome. And that is the purpose of this book: To provide you with easy-to-use strategies for managing information and the technologies that deliver it.

Three Steps to Managing Information

Before you can begin to manage information more effectively, you have to get personal. That is, you have to "browse" your most reliable "search engine," your greatest source of information—you!

Step 1: Identify Strengths, Admit Limitations

Begin by reviewing your strengths and weaknesses as they relate specifically to dealing with the information you handle every day. This exercise will help you to choose the management strategies described in this book that work best for you.

Start with the strengths (yes, you do have them). Do not bother with complete sentences; just jot down items in whatever form they come to you. For example:

➤ Fast reader

➤ Good at spotting important points in any document

➤ Enjoy learning new technology

My strengths:

_____

_____

_____

Sample weaknesses might include:

➤ Easily distracted; cannot concentrate when too much is going on

➤ Have trouble finding exactly what I need from Web searches

➤ Cannot coordinate paper and electronic materials

My weaknesses:

_____

_____

_____

Step 2: List Information Anxiety Relief Goals

The point of this step is to spell out and clearly identify what would make you feel better when it comes to managing information. Check (✔) those listed below that apply to you, and add as many others as you want.

❑ Learn how to find quality data and recognize useless information.

❑ Find a way to manage mail systems: Get rid of (or at least reduce) the amount of unwanted or unnecessary e-mail *(spam)*, voice mail, and junk paper mail.

❑ Do one thing at a time, and do it right, rather than do several things at once (multi-tasking) poorly.

❑ Unplug from some of the electronics in my life—at least some of the time.

❑ Dig out from the mountain of paper I'm under.

❑ Have enough time to think about and reflect on new information before making a decision.

❑ Separate "home" from "office." Limit the time I spend working, when I am supposed to be off, wherever I am.

❑ _____

❑ _____

❑ _____

Step 3: Rank Goals

From Step 2 above, list your five most important information anxiety relief goals, with the highest-priority goal first.

1. _____

2. _____

3. _____

4. _____

5. _____

Keep this list in mind as you go through this book. It will guide you in selecting the best tools and techniques. To help you meet your goals, this book covers each of these topics:

> ➤ **Multi-tasking**

> ➤ **Filtering information**

> ➤ **Managing messaging systems**

> ➤ **Processing paper**

> ➤ **Taming technology**

> ➤ **Telecommuting and working from home**

You can read these sections in any order, but it is a good idea to begin with the next part, on multi-tasking. Why? Because information overload leads most people to try to do too many things at once, or switch back and forth all the time. The result is a lack of focus, and the most important skill for information management is the ability to focus and be discriminating.

P A R T 2

Multi-Tasking

Is Multi-Tasking Really Such a Good Idea?

If you were planning to read this section at the same time you were going to catch up on the news on CNN, do yourself a favor: Turn off the TV and tune in here. Of course you are time-crunched, so you may think you have no choice but to get the information you need here at the same time you try to keep up with world events. But the truth is, if you try to do both, you will remember little of either. And that is the important point of this part: to open your eyes to the truth about multi-tasking.

In the past, people used to say, "She can't walk and chew gum at the same time" to describe someone who was not "smart enough" to be able to do more than one thing at a time. And you got the message, loud and clear: To succeed, you have to be able to juggle tasks—"to keep all the balls in the air."

The term *multi-tasking* was coined in 1966 to describe the capability of a computer to execute more than one task at the same time. Actually, the computer's central processing unit (CPU) switched from one program to another so quickly that it seemed to be executing all the programs at the same time.

When used to refer to people, however, multi-tasking has two meanings:

➤ Doing more than one thing at the same time

➤ Switching back and forth among several tasks, quickly and repeatedly

In fact, humans have been multi-tasking much longer than any machine. Just talk to any parent. But never before have people been expected to do so much at the same time, day in and day out with no respite, in an attempt to keep up with today's avalanche of information and the work it generates. Keeping up has become so onerous that it is getting people down. There is no question about it: Multi-tasking is not working.

COUNTING THE COSTS OF MULTI-TASKING

Maybe you are protesting: "Multi-tasking is working for me—I do it every-day." Of course you do; who doesn't? The question is, are you getting the results you would like when you do? To find out if multi-tasking is really working for you—or just making more work for you—answer *yes* or *no* to the following questions:

Do you ever have to reread your e-mail because, for example, you were talking on the phone at the same time you read it the first time, so you do not have a clue what it said?	❑ Yes ❑ No
Have you lost, misplaced, or misfiled an important document because you were talking on the phone or thinking about your next task when you filed it?	❑ Yes ❑ No
Have you ever had to lie to someone because you failed to fulfill a promise you made when you were not paying attention?	❑ Yes ❑ No
Do you sense your productivity dropping? Have you been making more errors lately? Do you have several projects underway, but cannot seem to complete any of them?	❑ Yes ❑ No
Do you have to repeat tasks because you do not do them right the first time because your mind is on something else?	❑ Yes ❑ No
Do you have more trouble concentrating these days? (Do you have to reread the same paragraph over and over because your mind keeps wandering?)	❑ Yes ❑ No
Are you more forgetful? Does everything seem to "go in one ear and out the other?" Do you make jokes to cover up?	❑ Yes ❑ No
Do you get frustrated more easily? Do you lose (or barely control) your temper over small matters or disagreements?	❑ Yes ❑ No
Do you feel guilty about the way you are doing your job or treating your friends and family, because you never seem to "be there," wherever "there" is?	❑ Yes ❑ No
Do you feel like a failure no matter how hard you work, how hard you try?	❑ Yes ❑ No

CONTINUED

---CONTINUED---

Do social opportunities feel more like obligations—another thing to do by a certain time? Are you distracted when in social situations because you are thinking about uncompleted work?	❑ Yes ❑ No

Did you answer *yes* to three or more of these questions? If so, you should now realize that just because you *can* multi-task does not mean you *should*. The issue is not the occasional instance of multi-tasking. It is the constant, unending, no-relief-in-sight grind that is getting to you and most of those you work with.

What the Experts Say

If you are still not convinced that multi-tasking is not a good way to get things done, maybe some scientific proof will change your mind. Psychologists and efficiency experts have been studying multi-tasking for many years and the results cannot be argued: Multi-tasking is not effective.

In one recent study by the U.S. Federal Aviation Administration (FAA) in conjunction with the University of Michigan, researchers measured the time it took subjects to perform and switch between varied tasks of increasing complexity. The study showed that multi-tasking may seem more efficient on the surface but may take more time in the end.

In a study by Carnegie Mellon University, psychologists used magnetic resonance images (MRIs) of brain activity to compare what happens during performance of a single task and then during multi-tasking. They discovered that rather than brain activity doubling when people tried to do even two things at once, the activity devoted to each task dropped.

Thus, the two independent studies came to remarkably similar conclusions:

➤ Doing several things at the same time reduces, rather than increases, productivity.

➤ Depending on the tasks, the outcome of multi-tasking can be dangerous. The classic example is driving and talking on a cell phone—even if it is a hands-free device.

➤ Multi-tasking does not save time; it costs time—as much as 20–40% in efficiency and accuracy, plus time lost due to switching between tasks. And time costs rise higher with the complexity of the task.

➤ Multi-tasking is not an efficient use of brainpower. Brain activity does not double when people try to do two things at once. That is, people doing two tasks at the same time do neither task as well as if they did each one alone.

What do these findings mean for you, the multi-tasker? They mean there has to be a better way. And there is, as you will find in the following sections.

Five Steps Out of the Multi-Tasking Maze

Despite multi-tasking's downsides, the goal is not to eliminate the practice altogether. The simple fact is that multi-tasking probably cannot be avoided altogether in today's high-tech, 24/7 world. There just aren't any surefire, easy-to-use strategies you can use to replace multi-tasking and still get everything done that you need to.

But multi-tasking can be managed through the following five-step process:

Step 1: *Estimate Task Times Accurately*

Step 2: *Give Your Brain a Break*

Step 3: *Limit Interruptions*

Step 4: *Concentrate*

Step 5: *Multi-task Smart*

Applying these five steps will help you find your way out of the multi-tasking maze. The next sections look at each of these steps in more detail.

Step 1: Estimate Task Times Accurately

Most people underestimate how long it takes to manage information—especially those repetitive tasks they do several times a day, almost without thinking (part of the problem!) such as opening mail, responding to messages, making copies, sending faxes, and the like. When was the last time you set aside time on your daily schedule to return calls? See, that time is not free.

Do you feel frustrated at the end of the day partly because of miscalculating how long things take? To find out, take a quick diagnostic Task Time Trial, adapted from *Context* magazine (Fall 1998), following these steps:

1. Schedule one day for the trial—ideally a typical day, not one with more than the usual number of meetings, or a new-client lunch date, or with a major deadline looming.

2. Make a list of all the tasks you plan to accomplish during those hours.

3. Write down how long you think each task will take.

Time Yourself

Now find out how accurate your time estimates were. With your task list nearby:

1. Note the time you start and finish the task.

2. Compare the times you wrote down with the actual time it took to do each task.

3. Figure out the difference. (See sample chart on the next page.)

4. Adjust your schedule to fit the more realistic time frame. This alone will help to reduce your frustration and will go a long way toward making you feel more productive and in better control.

Sample Task Time Trial

Task	Estimated Time to Complete	Actual Time to Complete	Difference
Read, respond to e-mail	25 minutes	120 minutes	95 minutes
Listen, respond to voice mail	15 minutes	25 minutes	10 minutes
Open and review paper mail	30 minutes	45 minutes	15 minutes
Read internal company memos, transmittals	10 minutes	15 minutes	5 minutes
Answer incoming phone calls	30 minutes	60 minutes	30 minutes
TOTAL Time Difference	110 minutes	265 minutes	155 minutes, or more than 2.5 hours

This exercise should help you to understand why you can have a to-do list that you never manage to complete. You probably have forgotten to allow time for three things:

➤ Unexpected interruptions

➤ Returning calls

➤ Responding to e-mail

Taking these tasks into account will help you develop more realistic expectations of what you can accomplish in a day.

Step 2: Use a To-Do List

If you are beginning to suffer from CRS (Can't Remember Stuff), then make your life easier. Stop making yourself remember things you do not have to.

Rather than juggling in your head all the tasks you have scheduled for the day, make a to-do list. This is a simple, fast, and effective tool. This tried-and-true strategy still works. For starters, it automatically reduces your memory load and helps you sleep better at night. Setting priorities is easier when you can see everything at one time on a single list.

To-Do List How-To's

No blizzard of sticky notes, please. Why? If you have sticky notes, plus a computerized to-do list, plus another list on paper—not to mention a couple of piles of active papers—you have too many places to look. When this occurs, it is easy to just do the next thing that comes to mind rather than the most important. And worse, if you have been away from your desk for a while, you are probably going to check your e-mail and get sucked in again.

Jot your to-do list on a piece of paper that you carry with you at all times. If you are disciplined about immediately adding items to an electronic to-do list, that is fine, but most people end up reaching for a sticky note, and the task never gets transferred to the electronic format.

Whichever system you use, keep in mind the following do's and don'ts:

Do:

➤ Use only one system. If you use both a paper and electronic planner, you will have to update and track in two places—which makes more work.

➤ Make separate lists of long-term and short-term tasks.

➤ Check off tasks as you accomplish them.

➤ Add new tasks promptly.

➤ Train yourself to write notes directly onto your list the first time.

Don't:

➤ Put more on the list than you know you can accomplish each day. It will only frustrate you.

➤ Post the list where you cannot see it or where it will become "invisible" in a day or two.

➤ Forget to refer to your to-do list.

➤ Use a sticky note for items that should go on your list.

Drafting Your List

You may choose to prepare your to-do list at the beginning or end of the day—or both—again depending on how you like to work:

➤ Are you a morning person? If so, consider coming into your office or workspace 10 minutes earlier, while it is still quiet, to make your list.

➤ Do you think more clearly at the end of the day? If so, leave time before you "close up shop" each day to prepare the next day's to-do list. Or stay a little later. Ten minutes is not very long if it relieves you from worry and enables you to plan your next day so you will not wake up in the middle of the night thinking about what you have forgotten.

➤ Do you prefer to cover both bases? If so, at the end of each day you can review what you have accomplished and get a jump-start on the next day's list by carrying over anything that was not completed.

If you find you are carrying over too many tasks each day, review Step 1 on estimating task times. Probably you are still underestimating how long things will take to accomplish.

If your log shows that you objectively have more tasks to do than there are hours in the day, you have a workload or volume problem, not a simple efficiency problem. If you are behind now and no new people are going to be hired, you must do something or eventually you will dedicate all your personal time to work, with no more to give. If the load is unmanageable, the best strategy is to:

1. Document the situation

2. Analyze the results

3. Negotiate with your manager

4. Set clear expectations about what you can and cannot do

Step 3: Limit Interruptions

A study by the Institute for the Future reported that employees of Fortune 1000 companies send and receive, on average, 178 messages a day and are interrupted about three times an hour. Sound like anyone you know? Remember that electronic interruptions are self-inflicted. The problem is not that you received an e-mail. The problem is that you allowed yourself to stop what you were doing to respond to the unknown, unexpected message that may or may not be a higher priority than what you were already doing.

When you limit interruptions, you help to control when and how often you tackle information management tasks. Try the suggestions below and feel free to adapt and add to this list to fit your work style and work life. Because you cannot change too much at once, select one or two on which to concentrate for a week. Then decide which will help you be more productive. Change them as necessary and try again, until you are working more efficiently.

Tips for Limiting Interruptions

➤ Read and respond to voice mail and e-mail only three times a day: upon arriving at your computer, after lunch, and a half hour before you quit for the day.

➤ Read and file paper documents and mail once a day. See Part 5, Processing Paper.

➤ Make copies and send faxes once a day.

➤ Browse the Web and download or print pertinent information once a day, preferably at a "quiet" time.

➤ Remove piles of paper. Clutter serves as a distraction just as surely as a person calling your name does.

Step 4: Concentrate

Let's say you have an important report to write by the end of the week, but every time you start to work on it, the phone rings, your e-mail alert pops up, and people keep coming in to your office. You know you need to focus, but you just cannot—there is too much going on.

No, you are not losing your mind. Experts say that memory loss (a normal brain function, by the way) increases when your mind is overloaded with information. This is especially true if you are trying to force it to switch between dissimilar tasks—one proactive, such as writing, and the other reactive, such as answering the phone or responding to a co-worker's question.

If you commit to using the following concentration tips when you need to focus on an important, time-sensitive task, your productivity is sure to improve:

Tips for Concentrating

➤ Hang a "do not disturb" sign on your door or outside your cubicle. Post a paper clock, the way small shops do, indicating when you will be "back." Or close your door.

➤ When working on your computer, close as many programs as you can, especially e-mail. When not working on your computer, turn off all programs except your screensaver.

➤ Turn off the audible indicator that a new e-mail has arrived.

➤ Turn off the ringer on the telephone. And, if you cannot stop looking to see if the light is blinking, cover the indicator.

➤ Turn off your cell phone and pager, if you have them. However, if your position requires off-hours availability, confirm with your manager exactly what that entails.

➤ If all else fails, find a distraction-free place to work. Perhaps a conference room or an absent co-worker's desk.

➤ Ask your manager if you can work at home for a day or two, until you finish the project. If you already work at home, run away: Go to the library, for example. And leave your phone and pager at home, or limit the times you will respond by checking three or four times a day rather than reacting the instant they go off.

Step 5: Multi-Task Smart

Have you ever gotten really irritated because you could tell that the person you were talking to on the phone was not paying attention? Maybe you could hear the clacking of computer keys in the background as he continued to work. Or the person took too long to answer a question you asked and only "tuned back in" when she realized you had stopped talking.

The point is, if you can tell, and you find it annoying, others can and do too. Again, multi-tasking is a part of life these days, but you have to be smart about when it works for or against you.

Tips for Smart Multi-Tasking

> **Use common sense.** It is probably okay to talk to your best friend on the phone while you are washing the dishes (if your friend does not mind the banging and splashing). But it is not a good idea to browse your e-mail while your manager is giving you instructions for a new project.

> **Monitor your progress.** You can tell when you are, or are not, working effectively. As soon as you start making errors, getting frustrated, or losing concentration because you are doing too many things at once, switch into single-task mode. You will get more done in the long run.

> **Be true to yourself.** You know how you prefer to work, the way in which you work most effectively. Do not compare yourself to the guy in the next office who seems to thrive on pressure and stress, and thrills to the challenge of keeping many balls in the air.

> **Count results, not attempts.** Is it better to finish two out of three tasks one at a time, or not complete anything? Remember, if there is time to do it over again to fix an error, there was the time to do it right initially.

> **Give yourself credit.** Why do we focus on the few items left uncompleted at the end of the day and ignore all that we did accomplish? Focus on the results. Make it a standing item on your to-do list to pat yourself on the back for all you do achieve every day. Just reminding yourself that you did get things done (even if not all you wanted or intended) will go a long way toward lifting your spirits, boosting your self-confidence, and giving you the energy to begin again tomorrow.

Filtering

Information

26

Balancing Your Data Diet

Imagine all the information available to you today as a gigantic all-you-can-seek information buffet, offering everything you could want and then some. There is so much to look at, you hardly know where to begin. So you just start adding things to your "plate," willy-nilly, until it is overflowing, spilling over everywhere. You know you have taken too much, and you know you cannot possibly digest it all, not without making yourself sick. But you do not want to throw any of it away either. It all looks so good, so relevant, so important.

But is it? Hardly. One of the reasons people take too much from the information buffet is that it is difficult to figure out what has "nutritional" value. This is because the focus of the Information Age has been on developing the resources for gathering data and not nearly enough on the really important job of converting the data into useable information.

As you read through this part, keep in mind what Paul Kaufman, an information theorist, says on the subject: "Too much attention has been focused on computers and hardware and too little on the people who actually use information in order to make sense of the world and do useful things for each other. The problem is not that we think so highly of computers, but that we've come to think rather less of humans."

Information You Get vs. Information You Use

Do you have any idea, really, how many sources of information you tap into every day? Have you ever stopped to think about how much time you spend "connected" to each? To get a handle on this important personal statistic, fill in the information buffet table below. This insight will prove invaluable as you proceed through this part.

A Day at the Information Buffet

Source	Time Spent	Source	Time Spent
Television		Newspaper(s)	
The Internet/Web		Magazine(s)/journal(s)	
Radio		Telephone(s)	
E-mail		Pager	
Voice mail		Personal digital assistant (PDA)	
Paper mail (including junk mail, catalogs)		Computer(s)	
Movies/videos		Books	
Meetings/conferences		Memos/faxes	
Other:		Other:	
	TOTAL:___		TOTAL:___

Next ask yourself how many hours (minutes?) a day you can count as quiet time, time you allow yourself to review, think about, evaluate (that is, convert) all that incoming data into information you can, and will, really use:

Daily quiet time: _____

Now do the math:

Hours gathering information − Hours converting information into useful knowledge = _____

If there is a big difference between these two figures (and for most people there is), it is time to ask yourself:

> ➤ What good is all this information if I am not using it, or do not have time to use it?

> ➤ How can I turn all that data into "nutritional" information and have more free time?

The first question is easy to answer: no good. The second question takes a little more work. And a good place to start is by figuring out how you define quality information. The pages that follow address this conundrum.

Identifying Quality Information

Quality information is defined as information that is relevant and valuable to you, that actually informs you.

➤ What makes information meaningful to you? (For example: "When it helps me do my job or improves my quality of life." "When it is easy to find and easy to understand.")

➤ How would you describe your ideal information? ("It is timely and accurate." "It is from a reliable source, easy to find and manage.")

➤ What would give you the most immediate relief from information frustration? (For example: "Less e-mail, especially the junk.")

➤ What would bring you more long-lasting relief from information frustration? (For example: "To stop feeling that I have to be constantly connected, no matter where I am and what else I am doing.")

With these questions in mind, write your own three to five criteria for quality information on the lines that follow:

_____

_____

_____

_____

_____

If you are having trouble coming up with your criteria, consider how Lynn Lively, in her book *Managing Information Overload,* defines ideal information:

> ➤ **Current:** timely; the latest version available

> ➤ **Sufficient:** enough to do your job well. (Lively recommends that you forget *complete*. "There's no such thing," she points out, and "even if there were, you wouldn't have the time or money it would take to get complete information.")

> ➤ **Essential:** what you must have to do your job and make your decisions

> ➤ **Reliable:** accurate and trustworthy

> ➤ **Verifiable:** reproducible—what other prudent people would come up with if they were doing the same thing you did

Making Distinctions

Although everyone uses the terms *information, data,* and *knowledge* interchangeably these days, in fact there are differences among them, differences that might help you to better filter information.

See if you can match up these terms with their correct definitions. (The correct answers are at the bottom of the page.*)

1. Data   a. Material organized into meaningful content

2. Information   b. Raw facts and figures

3. Knowledge   c. Organized data

The point of this quiz is not to teach you to use the terms properly when you speak or write.

What is important is that you recognize that *information is not the same as knowledge.*

*1. Data, is b; 2. Information, is a; 3. Knowledge, is c.

Limiting Your Information Gathering

Studies indicate that people never use 80% of the information they keep. That is a staggering statistic. If you are like most people, it means that more than three-quarters of the information you gather and perhaps even file is waste. And if you also think about the time you spent gathering that information—well, you see the point: You need to cut back.

Most companies have records-retention policies to help employees let go of what "might" become useful later. Much personal hoarding is not about official data. It is about the vague belief that you could conceivably need this or that item again before you retire. Ask yourself if saving everything for that rare occasion is worth the time and effort—keeping in mind that most tossed items are replaceable.

To do that, review the following guidelines and think about how you might apply them to the information sources you filled in on the information buffet table. You might even want to complete another table, but replace the "Time Spent" column with "Time Saved" once you have cut back or eliminated some of the sources.

Warning: You may find many of these suggestions difficult to implement, especially if you have become an "information junkie."

> **Reduce the number of hours you watch television.** You might as well start with the toughest one first. Think about it: Do you really want (or want your children) to spend five to eight hours a day (the average in American households) watching programs whose content you have no control over, other than the power switch and channel changer—even if it is CNN or C-SPAN? Is it worth the time you take away from other pursuits? It is a question of balance, not an either/or option.

> **Cut back on the number of newspapers and magazines to which you subscribe.** Cancel subscriptions for those you barely or never glance at anymore, whether paper or electronic versions. It is better to read fewer journals or magazines thoroughly than to have piles of them unread, gathering dust, and making you feel guilty. (See Part 4, Managing Messaging Systems, and Part 5, Processing Paper, for more on this.)

> In his book *Eight Weeks to Optimum Health,* acclaimed nutritionist Dr. Andrew Weil suggests taking what he calls a "news fast"—a period of time without reading, watching, or listening to any news. His point is not to become uninformed, but to learn to control the information you take in, to reduce anxiety, stress, and frustration.

➢ **Get off Internet time.** Being on "Internet time"—that is, 24/7—gives you a false sense of urgency and increases stress. Instead, put the Internet (including e-mail) on your schedule. Do this at home (especially if you have children) and at work. (More strategies for these topics can be found in Part 4, Managing Messaging Systems, and Part 6, Taming Technology.)

➢ **Monitor your phone time.** Just because the phone is ringing does not mean you have to answer it. Do not interrupt dinner with your family or friends, and do not pick up if you are ready to go to bed. For the cell phone that has become part of your body, be reasonable. You do not have to take it everywhere. Leave it at home or at least turn it off, such as when you are exercising, at the movies, in transit, in a meeting, out on a date, on vacation. You get the idea.

➢ **Disconnect electronics.** Learn to turn off your computer, ideally at a specific time each day. This will help you commit to stopping work, especially if you work from home or often take work home with you. And unless there is a very good reason (e.g., you are a doctor on call), turn off your pager and cell phone too. (More on this topic is in Part 6, Taming Technology.)

Using Information Filters

Keeping in mind that most people do not use 80% of the information they gather, the bottom line here is clear: You simply have to reject more information than you accept. But how do you know what to reject?

To help you figure it out, first refer to the criteria you developed for quality information. Keep these in mind because your goal is to filter out information that does not qualify as quality. To reach this goal, you need to apply information-filtering capabilities—your own and those offered by most electronic data resources today. This section discusses these filters.

Install E-Mail Filters

For many people, e-mail is the major source of information overload and frustration in their daily lives. So just by limiting junk e-mail—spam—and better managing the e-mail you have to accept, you will go a long way toward easing e-mail overload. This important topic is covered in depth in Part 4, Managing Messaging Systems. But here are two quick examples:

> ➤ **Put the *Spaminator* on the case.** Most e-mail programs today offer a spam filter, whether it is called the Spaminator or something similar. Turning it on is usually as simple as checking a box on your Internet home page. For help, (1) call your Internet service provider, (2) ask a friend or colleague with the same program, or (3) click on the *Help* button in your e-mail program. If your e-mail program does not offer this option, or you want a more high-powered filter, many are available for download from other online sources. See Part 4.

> ➤ **Do not give yourself away.** In the same way (multiplied millions—maybe billions—of times) that your contact information is sold to other mailing lists for the paper catalogs and junk mail that clog your mailbox, your e-mail address is passed to countless dot-coms in cyberspace. Think carefully before you automatically fill in your e-mail address every time it is requested on the Web.

Fine-Tune Search Engine Use

To untangle yourself from the ever-expanding Web, you have to learn—then use—effective search techniques. Because every search engine is different, it is not possible to detail engine-specific search strategies here. But a good way to find one that works for you is to do the following:

> ➤ **Comparison shop search engines.** Read the search hints or tips section of two or three search engines. A good place to start is www.metacrawler.com, which is recommended by several search-engine experts.

> ➤ **Run a test.** Choose a topic to research, then test the search engines you have chosen using the querying hints they recommend. Run the test on information you actually need—such as finding travel tips for an upcoming vacation. Compare the quality and quantity of information you receive. Do the results meet your criteria for quality information?

> ➤ **Bookmark reliable resources.** When you determine your favorite search engine(s), bookmark it. In the same way, bookmark valuable and reliable Web sites. Use the bookmark option on your browser.

> Tip: Add a library or two to your bookmarks. Once upon a time, that is where everyone went to do research. And in many cases today, libraries are still the best place to go for reliable information. Many of the best in the country—including the Library of Congress—make it possible to tap their resources via the Web.

> ➤ **Do not confuse quantity with quality.** With the Internet, more often means too much, resulting in more work and frustration. Who needs—or wants—10,000 or 1 million hits from a query when the Top 10 is what you are looking for? Once you learn to refine your search queries and use a search engine that is compatible with your way of working, you will find that less is more—and better too.

Be Your Own Editor

This has nothing to do with grammar and punctuation but everything to do with cutting and deleting—in this case, reducing the amount of incoming. Add the following cutbacks to your information management diet and you will start seeing the results in a leaner in-box.

➤ Unsubscribe to listservs, newsgroups, newsletters, and the like that you voluntarily signed on to receive but never read. Although you may have subscribed to such publications with the best of intentions, if they now serve only to clutter your in-box, forcing you to take time to delete them every time they are delivered, it is time to reverse your decision.

Warning: It is rarely as easy to get off an electronic mailing list as it was to get on it. But as with money, sometimes you have to spend time to make time. Follow the Unsubscribe links (they may be at the bottom, in small print) until you reach the end—that is, until you are off the list. Another option is to save a few weeks' worth of these unwanted e-mails in a specially labeled folder and then assign the task of unsubscribing to another person. This could be an assistant, a temp you hire for half a day, your best friend's teenager, or your own child. Be creative.

➤ Cut back on cable. As with search engine "hits," ask yourself: Is more better here? Do you just find yourself endlessly "channel surfing" for something decent to watch? Doesn't it seem there is just more to avoid (such as infomercials)? Why not save time—and money—and cut the cable? Or at least go back to basics: Sign up for the fewest channels at the lowest cost.

➤ Follow the Golden Rule. Do not send to others what you know you would not want to receive yourself. Simply, this means do not add to the information overload of others. Good information-management manners are catching: If you practice them, others will follow them.

Sorting the Information to Keep

Not only do people not use most of the information they gather, but they also spend approximately 150 hours a year looking for misplaced information they do need. If you do not use most of what you gather, then cannot find the information you do need, it is no wonder you are slowly, or rapidly, losing control.

Besides filtering incoming data, you also need ways to sort and store the information you do want and need. This part covers specific sort-and-store strategies for e-mail and paper. But for filtering purposes, you should ask four simple questions for every piece of information you handle:

1. Do I really need to keep this? (If yes, why? That is, make sure there is a very good reason.)

2. Where should I keep it? (In which format—paper or electronic? Stored in a file or a binder?)

3. How long should I keep this? (Separate permanent files from historical materials and regularly remove outdated documents.)

4. How can I find it when I need it? (If you are constantly asking yourself, "Now, where'd I put that...?" you need to rethink your system. It has to be so obvious to you that you almost don't have to think at all about where to find it.)

Staying on Your Data Diet

If you have ever been on a food diet, you know there are a million reasons (excuses, really) for falling off. It is the same on the data diet. You will be pressured by deadlines, competition, peers, interruptions, self-doubt, you name it. The following are some final tips that can help when you feel yourself giving in to an information binge—trying to take in too much in too short a time:

➤ **Just say, "I don't know."** This is as important an information-filtering strategy as any. No one can keep up with the deluge of information today, so give yourself permission not to know. The next time someone asks for your input about material that you have not had time to read, be brave; do not fudge or fib. Say something like: "Sorry, I haven't had a chance to review that yet, but I'd be interested in hearing what you think." (Chances are the questioner has not yet read it either and was hoping to pass the buck!)

➤ **Change your information filters as necessary.** Your information needs change; do not forget to change your resources to match. If you change jobs or are working on a new project, or the search engine you have been using is not giving you quality information lately, take the time to revamp your filtering strategies. Again, sometimes you have to spend time to make time.

➤ **Walk away.** When you feel the frustration building and you feel you may collapse under the onslaught, take a break. Even a short time-out will give you a new perspective. Believe it: You cannot afford not to take a break.

For in-depth instructions on sorting and filing paper, read *Organizing Your Workspace,* also by Odette Pollar, A Crisp book by Thomson Learning.

PART 4

Managing

Messaging Systems

40

Taking Control

Do you have a love-hate relationship with your voice mail and e-mail, your primary messaging systems? When you first began to use those systems, no doubt the relationship was more love than hate. You loved the freedom and flexibility these systems promised.

But after spending some time living and working together, the relationship began going downhill—fast. Lately you have begun to feel trapped by, even controlled by, the constant connectivity these systems seem to require. Where is the freedom? Where is the flexibility?

It is still there, but it is up to you to reclaim it. You have to control the systems, not let the systems control you. This chapter tells you how, beginning with the messaging system that has become a major cause of anxiety and frustration: e-mail.

Evaluating Your Use of E-Mail

It is not surprising that millions of users feel buried under an avalanche of e-mail. This messaging system swept down the technology mountain so fast and furiously that few anticipated the impact it would have.

And what an impact. In 2001, according to International Data Corporation, more than 1.4 trillion e-mail messages were sent by North American businesses (up from 40 billion in 1995). Internet users received an average of more than 700 spam messages in 2001 (expected to climb to 1,500 by 2006). Workers spend from one to four hours a day handling their messages, 80% of which many consider a waste of time.

To extricate yourself, you need strategies to improve your current e-mail handling. But before you do that, you must figure out how you are currently processing e-mail. In this context, *processing* does not mean opening a message, reading it without taking action, and leaving it in your in-box. What it does mean is outlined in the three-step process that follows.

Step 1: Pinpoint the Process

Schedule a quiet time when you can both read your e-mail and monitor what you do. As you go through your in-box, note the steps you take and jot them on the lines below. Use as many lines as you need to describe this process. Thirty messages should give you enough data. The first entries below are samples to get you started. HINT: Use action verbs, such as open, read, delete, file, print, archive, and the like.

1. Read sender names and header files to gauge importance.

2. Automatically delete messages that are clearly spam, promotionals, or newsletters I never read anymore.

3. Open message from the boss, realize it is too long to deal with now, close it, and make a mental note to return to it later.

4. Open message related to an earlier e-mail, skip new messages to find earlier one.

5. _____

6. _____

Was there a rhyme and reason to your process, or did you notice a lot of "backing-and-forthing"?

Step 2: Identify Points of Failure

From what you learned in Step 1, specify where you are getting tripped up in those steps. Check the boxes below that you can relate to:

❑ To get through all my messages, often I just skim them. The result is that sometimes I overlook what's important.

❑ Frequently, I will open a message, realize I do not have time to deal with it, promise myself to get back to it, then never do.

❑ I deal with spam by not dealing with it—that is, I spend time every day deleting it, rather than finding a more lasting solution.

❑ I "click away" newsletters, newsgroups, and so on. I signed up for these things, but don't have time or don't want to be involved with them anymore.

❑ I grumble every time I'm copied on an e-mail or included in a group message (especially a Reply to All) that I do not need to receive.

❑ I get frustrated, even angry, every time someone sends me a slow-to-download graphics file.

❑ I get too many jokes.

❑ I get annoyed when I get questions from people that were clearly answered in my last e-mail to them—meaning they did not take the time to read it carefully so I now have to take the time to deal with it again.

❑ I have heard and read about new programs or features that would help ease my e-mail overload, but I haven't taken the time to study them.

❑ Sometimes it is days before I respond to messages, and it is starting to have a negative impact on my relationships. I do this even though I resent it when other people do it to me.

❑ I rarely—or never—clean out, file, or archive old messages. I have hundreds of outdated e-mails that have taken up permanent residence in my in-box.

❑ Despite my frustration with the e-mail I get, I know I'm guilty of causing others the same problems.

❑ I have no patience for the round-robins that happen when someone tries to schedule a meeting with several people via e-mail, resulting in a flurry of messages but no decision.

Step 3: Take a Time Test

See how much time you are spending on unproductive e-mail actions. HINT: For this exercise, complete one task at a time, such as deleting spam, and make note of your start and end times for each.

Time Test

Action	Time Started	Time Finished
Delete spam		
Read/respond to messages I really didn't need to receive		
Be held hostage by graphics-heavy, slow-to-download "joke" files sent by well-meaning friends and colleagues		
"Recycle" newsletters I subscribed to but no longer read		
Scroll through long lists of old messages I've never archived to find the new message		
Other:		

Just completing each of these actions a couple of times will show you two things:

➤ The increasingly large chunks of time you spend that you evaluate as wasted

➤ The relatively short amount of time it takes to make permanent changes, such as removing yourself from lists or setting up a spam filter, which result in lasting time and energy savings

Tip: It's Not Funny

If you hate getting joke e-mails, especially the slow-to-download graphics form, tell your friends that your company has a policy that does not permit handling personal matters over the system at work. Ask them not to send any more jokes. This will take the heat off you.

Easing E-mail Congestion

To handle e-mail effectively, you must implement a system—and then use it religiously. Most effective e-mail-handling strategies will include the seven actions that follow. You do not have to follow the sequence listed here. Change the order as you see fit to suit the way you like to work.

Action 1: Get to know your e-mail program. If you have never taken the time to explore the features your e-mail program offers, this must be your first step. At a minimum, you should:

> ➤ Review organizing and filing options. Learn how to set up action folders or use color-coding.

> ➤ Find out about easy-to-install filters that allow messages to automatically go into identified folders.

> ➤ Learn how to automate repetitive tasks, such as including contact information.

> ➤ Learn how to archive.

> ➤ Learn how to turn off the audible alarm alerting you to incoming messages.

Action 2: Schedule and limit e-mail checks. Twice a day is ideal. By limiting e-mail checks, you will quickly realize you need not read your e-mail the instant it arrives. The reduction in stress alone will make this step worthwhile. Disabling the e-mail buzzers, beeps, and pop-up alerts that interrupt you to tell you a new message has arrived will help you stick to your e-mail schedule.

Action 3: Scan→sort→decide. Choose whatever categories work for you. Options include by subject line, by original or copied-on messages, by sender name. Decide quickly how to handle each message, then act on your decision: answer it, file it, delete it, and so on. Dilly-dallying and procrastinating are not options.

Some companies are implementing an e-mail "valuing" policy in which employees attach a value such as "Urgent" to the message subject. This makes sorting and ranking easier for everyone. For this to work, however, the parameters of "Urgent" must be clearly defined, or this system can be easily mis- and over-used.*

Action 4: Filter. In addition to the spam-filtering strategies yet to come, investigate "bozo filters." These are software programs that enable users to enter the names of people, companies, agencies, and others from whom they want (and do not want) to receive mail. Bozo filters are great for controlling "group" mailings.

Action 5: Unsubscribe. Review the newsletters and newsgroups you signed up for. If you are not reading or participating, follow the *Unsubscribe* links and get off those lists.

Action 6: Schedule cleanup and archiving. Regularly (at least once a month) clean out your in-box, folders, and trash (recycle) bin. If you do not, even the best e-mail system will collapse under the weight of old news.

Action 7: Disable the receipt of instant messages—IMs. If this feature is still on in your e-mail program, turn it off. These messages can be major distractions and interruptions.

---

* For more on e-mail policy-making and other e-mail help, visit www.epolicyinstitute.com. The ePolicy Institute is dedicated to helping companies develop and implement policies for safe and efficient e-mail and Internet use. Individuals too can find lots of help at this site. Check out the *Free Stuff* links, which include "Super-Effective Electronic Writing," "ePolicy Do's & Don'ts," and more.

E-Mail Do's and Don'ts

Make the following e-mail do's and don'ts an integral part of your e-mail process:

Do:

➤ Make it short and snappy. Limit your messages to a maximum of three sentences. If you have more than that to say, attach a word document with the full text, and alert the recipient that you are sending the attachment.

➤ Automate repetitive tasks. If you always include your contact information with e-mail, set up an electronic "signature." If you have a must-forward list by project, automate the procedure.

➤ E-mail to others as you would like others to e-mail to you.

➤ Be virus-vigilant. Be wary of e-mail from anyone you do not know or that contains an attachment you were not expecting. Update your antivirus software at least once a week.

➤ Fill in the subject line. Be specific and brief such as "Jordan proposal: client feedback," as opposed to "proposal feedback."

Don't:

➤ Be a copycat. Don't automatically *cc:* your colleagues and friends. Think first: Is it necessary? Don't hit the *Reply (*or *Reply All)* key on a group message if your response is only to the sender or select group members. Don't forward chain letters.

➤ Be lazy. Don't type in all caps (regarded as "shouting") or all lowercase letters. It may be faster for you, but it is more difficult for recipients to read.

➤ Schedule your e-mail checks during your breaks. If you do, it is not a break, and you need those.

➤ Hit *Reply* on an old subject line if the topic has changed. Start a new message if you are introducing a new topic. This helps your reader(s) to rank messages and helps you to track communications.

Reducing Spam

For many people, just emptying their in-box of spam can be a major time-saver. And there is a lot you can do, quickly and easily, to reduce the amount of junk you get. The key word here is "reduce," because as long as you use e-mail, you probably will not be able to eliminate spam entirely—it is, after all, a billion-dollar industry.

The Spam Dilemma

Spam, the electronic version of common mass-marketing practices, puts Internet service providers (ISPs) between a rock and a hard place: Spam marketers are a source of revenue for ISPs, but they are also a source of mounting user complaints.

To you, the user, spam seems more intrusive than other mass-marketing campaigns, for two reasons: (1) the vehicle used to drive it—the Internet—can move at unimaginable speeds, and (2) spam producers take a "shotgun," as opposed to targeted, approach to their mailings. This guarantees that most of the spam you receive will be of no interest to you.

According to Jason Catlett, president of Junkbusters, spam makes up 20–25% of all e-mail on the Internet. And, depending on your ISP, it could be more. The larger your ISP, the more spam you will get every day. For example, AOL users report that up to 33% of their e-mail is spam.

Four Actions for Reducing Spam

To get control of your spam problem, consider taking the following actions:

Action 1: Filter, filter, filter. For stopping spam in its tracks, the importance of filtering cannot be overstated. Here are three easy ways to help stop the spread of spam:

➤ Install a spam filter from your home page. Most ISPs make this possible with just a couple of mouse clicks. Go to your browser's home page and look for a button that reads something like "Stop Junk Mail." Click on it and follow the directions. If you do not see such an option, search the Help file on terms such as "spam," "junk mail," or "filter."

➤ Install a filter from your e-mail program. Many e-mail programs come with built-in spam filters that can be clicked into action. Or you can set up your own, more effective filter very easily. Each e-mail program has a different way to do this (typically via the Tools menu), so search the Help file under "filter" for directions.

➤ Purchase a commercial desktop spam-filtering program. These automate the spam-prevention process and can cost from $30 to $50.

Action 2: Stop spambots. Most spam-spreaders use a process called *harvesting* to capture e-mail addresses. The harvesting is done by a computer program called a *spambot* (robot→spambot, get it?) that automatically and continually prowls the Web for e-mail addresses. To prevent these spambots from getting your e-mail address in the first place:

➤ Set up an e-mail account just for use on the Web. Use this address when signing up for e-mail lists and newsgroups and on Web sites that request you to fill in an e-mail address.

➤ Do not reply to "unsubscribe" links in unsolicited (spam) messages. Doing so just sets you up for more spam. This is similar to letting telephone telemarketers get a word in edgewise.

Action 3: Ask for help. If you need more help than the preceding strategies can provide—for example, your home or children's computer is being bombarded with pornographic spam—there are several organizations you can contact:

➤ Coalition Against Unsolicited Commercial E-mail—CAUCE (www.cauce.org)—to track the progress of getting a federal spam law passed and to learn how to get involved

➤ Junkbusters (www.junkbusters.com)—for tips and tricks for stopping spam-spreaders

➤ Spamhaus (www.spamhaus.org)—to identify specific spam sources

➤ FBI Internet Fraud Complaint Center (www1.ifccfbi.gov)—to get help for serious problems caused by spamming

➤ Spam Laws (www. spamlaws.com)—to read about legislation on unwanted e-mail in easy-to-understand language

Action 4: Be part of the solution. The Federal Trade Commission (FTC) has a special spam "mailbox" where you can forward your unsolicited e-mail (www@ftc.gov). Since 1998 it has collected more than 10 million spam messages. The FTC uses the data compiled to supplement law enforcement and consumer and business education efforts.

Voice Mail Give and Take

For voice mail to be an effective helpmate in managing information, you have to give it as well as take it. It is the golden rule again: If you leave polite, timely, and concise messages, chances are that is what you will get in return.

Giving: Guidelines for Leaving Voice Messages

➤ Reserve voice mail for short, single-subject messages that do not require a paper trail.

➤ Limit your messages to between 20 seconds and two minutes, or you will "lose" your listener.

➤ State the purpose of your call briefly and clearly. If it is urgent, say so, but do not "cry wolf."

➤ Think about what you want to say before you call; write it down if that helps you be more concise.

➤ Tell the recipient specifically what you are looking for and how you would like the reply. Do you want a call back? Do you prefer e-mail? Are you expecting a fax?

➤ If you are making an important call on your cell phone, be sure you are in a good "reception" area. Do not risk annoying the person you are calling by getting disconnected or by speaking over street traffic or other interference.

➤ Do not answer your phone only to say, "I'll call you back." Let callers leave a message if you cannot talk when the phone rings.

Taking: Guidelines for Receiving Voice Messages

Strategies for answering voice mail are similar to those for handling e-mail.

➤ Use voice mail as it is intended, not to avoid people. Answer your telephone whenever you can. When you cannot, state in your greeting when you will check and reply to messages. If possible, tell callers how they can reach a "live" person for more urgent calls.

➤ Schedule regular voice mail checks. This is particularly important if you are traveling or just in and out of your office a lot. That said, do not check so often you make the task an interruption or a form of procrastination.

➤ Act on each message immediately. This is key to successful voice mail management. Reply, forward, save, or delete each message as soon as you have listened to it. If it represents a task, add it to your to-do list or calendar promptly.

➤ When you are busy, use caller ID as a form of voice mail filtering.

➤ Change your voice mail greeting daily. This lets callers know when to expect a return call.

Considering Instant and Unified Messaging

Messaging technologies are changing every day so it stands to reason that in the future you will need to adjust your message management strategies. Two technologies you might want to start with are instant messaging and unified messaging.

Instant messaging (IM) lets you see whether friends or co-workers are connected to the Internet and, if so, enables you to exchange messages with them in real time. (AOL and Yahoo users will already be familiar with IM.) IM differs from ordinary e-mail in that the message exchange is immediate (similar to a voice conversation, but using typing rather than speaking). Originally developed for personal interactions, it is being used more today to speed up business transactions.

The questions to ask yourself about IM are:

> ➤ Do I need or want to speed up communications even more—or will I just be going nowhere faster?

> ➤ Do I have the time to climb this learning curve?

The goal of *unified messaging* (UM) is to consolidate all your e-mails, voice mails, and fax messages in a single convenient place where you can receive, view, and organize all messages. UM processes voice, fax, and regular text messages as objects in a single mailbox that you can access either from a regular e-mail address or by telephone. UM holds particular promise for telecommuters and mobile businesspeople because it allows them to reach colleagues and customers through a PC or telephone, whichever is available. Sounds good, but this technology still has problems of compatibility among various applications.

The questions to ask yourself about UM are:

> ➤ If I implement the messaging management strategies given in this book, do I really need this technology now?

> ➤ Can I afford to wait until the compatibility issues are resolved?

It is a good idea to stay informed about what is new in this field, which you can do easily by using your Web browser to search on terms such as "messaging systems" and "message management."

At the Controls

By implementing the strategies in this part, you will find your relationship with your messaging systems improving immediately. Always keep in mind that you control the systems, not vice versa.

When you feel yourself losing that control, step back, review the techniques you learned, and start again. You may have to do this regularly, but now that you know how, it will become easier each time.

Do not fall off the wagon just because you went through an especially busy time or were away on a trip.

PART 5

Processing Paper

The Worsening Paper Pile-Up

Remember the paperless office? No, of course you don't. It never existed. It was a figment of the imagination of the so-called technology gurus, the folks who brought you the personal computer, the Internet, and the World Wide Web.

In fact, advances in technology have brought you more paper to deal with, not less. And here are the stats to confirm your feeling that things are getting worse:

➤ About 90% of the world's information is still on paper

➤ More than 10,000 newspapers and magazines are published in the United States alone

➤ Every year, more than 100,000 new books are published in the United States (more than a million worldwide)

➤ More than 60 billion pieces of junk mail are delivered to mailboxes every year

Did You Know?

The U.S. Post Office counts on junk mail for more than 90% of its revenue.

Add to those figures the untold quantities of work-related paper that pass over your desk and through your hands every day: memos, faxes, reports, plus e-mails and Web content you print out "to read later."

The point is, not only is paper alive and well, it has become a major cause of anxiety and overload, not to mention that it threatens to take over every vacant flat surface in your home and office.

Understanding Your Resistance to Proper Processing

A good place to begin regaining control is by identifying how paper piles up in the first place. Why do you think you push paper aside, rather than process it properly? Check (✔) which reasons in the following list apply to you and add any other reasons at the bottom:

❑ You have to wait for input, a decision, or approval from someone else before acting yourself

❑ You do not want to respond, or are not sure how to

❑ You have been away and have more important things to catch up on than your paperwork

❑ You do not have all the necessary information, or it is a new project that you are not sure how to handle

❑ _____

_____

_____

If you analyze the reasons that keep you from attacking paper pile-ups, you will see that generally, they fall into three categories:

➤ Fear of dumping

➤ Resistance to filing or lack of a workable filing system

➤ Lack of time

How legitimate are these reasons? Let's look at them one at a time.

Fear of Dumping

Most people say they do not throw away paper documents because they are sure that the minute they do, they will need or want it. But be honest: How often has this happened? Isn't it true that, generally, once you throw something away, you never miss it? When you compare reasons for tossing paper against reasons for saving it, you will quickly see that you should be dumping more paper more frequently than you do.

When to Save

➤ It is the only copy, and replication or replacement would be difficult

➤ It requires action on your part

➤ You know you will need to refer to the information again soon or regularly

➤ The law or office policy requires that you keep it

➤ It is an integral part of a project or client file

➤ It is necessary to keep a "paper trail;" that is, you must track every step or action in a project

When to Dump

➤ The information is a duplicate; someone else has it or it is filed elsewhere and is retrievable

➤ You simply want to keep it even if you do not really need to

➤ The information is outdated; it has been replaced by newer data

➤ The information has little or no relevance to your work or life

➤ You cannot identify any circumstances for which you would need the information

➤ It does not add significantly to existing material already on hand

➤ The information represents wishful thinking on your part— something you know you really will not have time to do

Note: In these tips, "dumping" generally means recycling. And if documents contain personal or confidential information (such as credit card or social security numbers), they should be shredded.

Resistance to Filing

To manage paper so that it becomes a source of usable information, rather than a cause of information anxiety, you will have to develop—and use—an effective filing system. (Stack-piling does not qualify as a form of filing—no matter how neat you make your piles or how high you can build them before they tip over.) Many people resist filing. Why? For "very good reasons" (read: excuses).

It is time to face the facts of filing—that is, to separate your reasons for not filing from the reality of what happens when you do not. Read the following "reason vs. reality" list. Can you add other excuses you use?

Reason (Excuse)	Reality
Out of sight is out of mind: If I file it, I'll forget about it.	You will forget about it anyway once it gets buried under a pile. And if you forget about it, you did not need to keep it in the first place.
I don't have time to file.	Yeah, right, but you do have time to go digging through the piles on your desk looking for that need-it-now document?
I can't remember where I file things.	Then your filing system is just a pile disguised in a folder. You need a system that works and a way to categorize or label things so you remember what you titled them and can easily retrieve them.
Files quickly become unmanageable, with too much stuff.	An easy fix: Schedule—and keep—file-purging appointments for yourself. How about the last Friday of every month?
Others:	

Lack of Time

The third reason for not attacking paper pile-ups is probably the most common—lack of time. It is also the easiest to refute logically. When you tell yourself now that you do not have time to file this memo or that report, what you also are saying is that you will have the time later to hunt for it—probably through even higher and more disorganized piles of paper.

Do the math: The time it takes you today to file something properly (usually mere seconds) is always less than the time it takes you to search for it (a half hour, hour, or more). If you are still telling yourself you do not have time to file, start telling yourself instead that you do not have time *not* to file. The next section will help you get into filing mode to prevent those paper pile-ups.

Developing an Effective File System

What exactly qualifies as an effective filing system? Well, the short answer is, one that works for you and is logical and easy to use.

Because everyone has different needs and requirements for accessing information on paper, it is impossible to design a one-size-fits-all filing system. Still, the following get-you-started guidelines can work for everyone:

1. Categorize files by subject (using things or items) or alphabetically (using names or places). (Note: Three other ways to categorize—numerical, geographical, and chronological—are generally unnecessary for personal files. Usually these are used for larger departmental or central files.)

2. Create working project files (for example, client or customer name, project title, contracts, etc.).

3. Create working administrative files (sample labels might include budget, expense reports, staff meetings).

4. Label with nouns (for example, "Contract Negotiations," not "How to Negotiate Contracts"). Avoid using adjectives or superfluous information.

5. File papers in broad categories. It is better to have thick files of related materials than numerous files with only a few pieces of paper in each one.

6. Divide all your files into three or four broad groupings. This lets you quickly identify what cabinet, drawer, or section a document is in. (These groups might represent the broad areas of responsibility.) Then alphabetize within each category. This makes retrieval faster and easier for you and for others.

7. File chronologically, with most current up front.

8. Use files within files to divide information within a single file.

Maintaining Your File System

Just as important as setting up a filing system is maintaining it. Follow these tips:

➤ **File regularly.** Thirty minutes twice a week will keep most filing under control.

➤ **Purge regularly.** A simple way to keep files clean and orderly is to purge as you file. That is, when you are adding something new to a file, check quickly at the back—the oldest information—to see if any of it can be removed at this time.

➤ **Always put new items up front.** Placing things in front means you will not have to search the entire file for a recent item.

Electronic Filing vs. Paper Files

Technological advances have added to the paper influx. As more information becomes available electronically, people find themselves printing out Web content, e-mails, and documents attached to e-mails. Whether they intend to read them later or they simply feel more comfortable with paper copies in their files, the simple fact is that electronic-source paper piles are on the rise. Here are some tips for managing paper of electronic origin:

➤ Rather than automatically printing electronic content, set up an electronic filing system. Perhaps set up two files: one in your e-mail program for messages you need to save (refer to Part 4, Managing Messaging Systems) and one in your word processing program for Web content you download for reference.

➤ Do not duplicate. Do not file documents both electronically and in paper files. Decide which is the more effective way to file each document so that it is most easily accessible.

➤ Print, then toss. If you must print an electronic file to read—for example, "on the road"—toss it when you are done. If you have made notes on the paper version, add the notes to the electronic file at the first opportunity.

➤ Schedule electronic file maintenance. Computer files can get out of hand as quickly as paper. Do not trade paper pile-ups for overstuffed electronic files. (Hint: Set the "Reminder" function in your e-mail program to tell you when it is time to do electronic file maintenance.)

For more in-depth information on filing, and for managing paper generally, read *Organizing Your Work Space,* also by Odette Pollar, A Crisp book by Thomson Learning.

Reducing Disposable Incoming Mail

One of the most effective ways to reduce paper pile-ups is simply to put a stop to *disposable incoming*. This includes everything you receive on paper that you regard as junk, defined as anything you toss, shred, recycle—that is, dump—almost as soon as you get it.

As with keeping spam out of your e-mail in-box, the idea of permanently and completely emptying your postal mailbox of junk is too much to hope for. But you are not entirely at the mercy of marketers either. You can significantly reduce the amount of junk mail you get now and in the future by making a consistent effort.

Identifying Junk Mail

The first step in eradicating disposable incoming from your mailbox is identifying what you consider it to be. List all the forms of junk mail you receive. You can start with the following list and add your own ideas:

➤ "Pre-approved" credit card offers

➤ Retail catalogs

➤ Retail sale flyers, coupons, and other "special offers"

➤ Charitable request mailings

➤ _____

_____

If you prefer, rather than making a list, just save all your junk mail in a container for a couple weeks, then go through the box and systematically dispose of the items using the strategies on the following pages.

Four Actions to Stop Junk Mail

Just taking the following stop-actions against the major four junk-mail perpetrators will be so effective that you will soon be psyched into doing more.

Stop-Action 1: Refuse credit card offers

Some people get 10 or more "pre-approved" credit card solicitations every week. To put a stop to these, you can either:

➤ Call each of the creditors individually, and tell them you want off their mailing list. (You may, however, have to use a magnifying glass to read the small print that tells you where and how.)

➤ Call the credit-reporting industry prescreening opt-out number, toll-free, 888-567-8688 to put a stop to them. (This service is supported by all credit agencies.)

Stop-Action 2: Cut back on catalogs

For a month (or a week, if you are really bombarded), stack up all the catalogs you get. Then set aside a couple hours one day (or a half hour every day for a week) and call the catalog companies and ask to be taken off their mailing list. Read the fine print, usually in the order form area of the catalog. More companies today are giving their customers the option to stop or reduce the frequency of mailings.

If you like to receive certain catalogs, but not every week or month, call the company and ask to receive, for example, holiday or sale mailings only.

Stop-Action 3: Ground sale flyers

Retailers like to think that your buying one item from them is the start of a beautiful friendship, when all you are interested in is a "one-buy stand." So when you are asked for your address and telephone numbers, refuse to give them. And don't worry, retailers will still take your money.

Stop-Action 4: Stop giving if it means more pleas for more money

If you support charitable or cultural organizations but resent being harassed by repeated mailings to give more, more, more, then a quick fix is to state your case to the organization: that you fully intend to send in your annual pledge, but that is it. Let the group know that you welcome a once-a-year reminder, but no more.

Tip: Go Direct

You may be able to kill several forms of junk mail with one stop-action: Contact the Direct Marketing Association (P.O. Box 9008, Farmingdale, NY 11735) and supply your name (in all forms that mail is addressed to you) and your home address. Ask that you be removed from all direct mailing lists with which the association is affiliated.

Creating New Ways to Reduce Paper Pile-Ups

Another effective strategy for reducing paper pile-ups is to imagine *if-then scenarios*. You will be amazed at the ways you can innovate to reduce the paper in your life. Here are examples of how this creative exercise works:

If...	Then...
You and one or more of your friends have subscriptions to the same magazines...	Start your own circulating library. Each of you buys a subscription to one magazine and passes it to the others. (This is a great strategy for self-employed people in the same line of work.)
Your company gets an office copy of the same newspaper you receive at home...	Cancel the one at home and read the paper at work during a break.
You only sometimes find the articles in a magazine or journal to which you subscribe interesting or useful...	Cancel the subscription, then once a week (or month, or however often the publication comes out), cruise your favorite newsstand and check out the table of contents. If you like what you see, buy it; if you do not, keep walking.
You subscribe at home to work-related publications...	Ask your manager to budget for office copies. If you are the manager, do it yourself. Then cancel your home delivery.
Your job or your curiosity requires that you read numerous publications regularly...	Head for your local library. Most subscribe to every publication you could ever want and then some. Or go Web surfing: Many publications make all or part of their content available online, some for a fee, some for free. (P.S. The Internet is also a good place to check on contents of current issues.)

Besides lowering your publication pile, the if-then scenario exercise also has the following benefits:

> **Cost savings.** One New York woman who formed a casual circulating library with her friends cut her annual subscription costs by three-fourths.

> **Keener eye for what is important.** When you no longer subscribe to publications, you learn to peruse them quickly at newsstands and elsewhere for what is interesting and important to you. Think of this process as the human version of the electronic filtering described in Part 3.

> **Relationship builder.** When you share subscriptions with like-minded friends and colleagues, you will find that they will point out items of interest to you, and you will do the same for them. It is fun and you will learn a lot.

Paper Wrap-Up

Finally, when you are faced with paper pile-ups and you do not know where to begin, jump-start the process by asking yourself these four simple questions:

➤ What is the worst thing that would happen if I tossed this? (Probably not much.)

➤ Where should I keep it? (In a file with related documents.)

➤ How long do I need to keep it? (Decide initially when it will no longer have value.)

➤ How can I remember where to find it? (What is a logical category to put this in?)

P A R T 6

Taming Technology

Mind Over Machine

It is not uncommon nowadays to hear the media refer to technology as a "beast" that has to be "tamed." For example, a tech report in *USA Today* (June 2000) read: "Engendering fear and sometimes loathing, technology has grown into an unwieldy beast." And one tech-watch author, Jason Ohler, even titled his book, *Taming the Beast: Choice and Control in the Electronic Jungle*.

Lee Rainie, director of the Pew Internet and American Life Project, which conducts an ongoing examination of the effects of technology on our lives, uses less dramatic language to describe the problem: "Technology is relentless," he says. "In the case of the average user, it seems as if there are new gizmos to master all the time."

But, as the *USA Today* article continues, "There are ways to tame [technology's] more exotic and intriguing species." And take note of the less attention-grabbing subtitle of Ohler's book: *Choice and Control in the Electronic Jungle*. The point is, we humans tend to take for granted all that technology has done to improve our lives, yet we waste no time in blaming it for the problems it causes and the challenges it presents. We forget that, to a great degree, we still can choose and control which technologies to use and how and when.

This part is about how to minimize frustration and maximize utility. Learning to make better choices about which technologies you use and how you use them is a two-part process:

1. Knowing what you have. This requires that you itemize all the technologies you already "share your life with" and assess how you use (or do not use) them.

2. Stopping before you shop. After identifying how the technologies you already own or use affect your life (either positively or negatively), you need to learn how to make informed decisions before you buy more.

Taking Stock of the Technologies You Have

Whether you realize it or not, you have been adapting to new technologies over a long time—years, in fact. This means that many of them have become such an integral part of your life that you may not even be aware of how much of your time and behavior is dictated by their use.

To get an accurate idea of how much technology surrounds you, divide a sheet of paper into two columns (or make a photocopy of the table below), then walk around your home and jot down each type of technology you find. If you have more than one of some items (for example, more than one television set, desktop computer, and phone, plus high-tech kitchen appliances), add a third column, labeled "Quantity."

If your "technostress" is more acute at your office, whether the office is in your home or elsewhere, you might want to make separate lists for each location.

The following table lists several popular technologies that many people own, but it is far from comprehensive. It does not include kitchen-related technologies, which you will want to add to ensure that you get a firm grasp of the role technology plays in your life.

Technologies I Own

Desktop Computer	Laptop Computer
Palm/Other Handheld	Fax machine
Scanner	Television
Color printer	Black-and-white printer
Photocopier	Cell phone
Cordless/wireline telephone	DVD player
Home audio system	CD player
Video game system	Portable audio system
Camcorder	Digital/film camera
Pager	VCR

If you buy or download a lot of software programs, think about including these on your list too. This is especially important if you, like many people, don't take the time to learn the programs' features, then end up not using them properly—or at all.

How Do You Use the Technologies You Own?

Having itemized the technologies you have, now you can begin to form a picture of whether you are making the best use of those technologies.

Divide a new sheet of paper into three columns:

Column 1: Technology. Use the list you developed in the preceding section.

Column 2: Intended Use. Note why you bought each item.

Column 3: Actual Use. Using the time frames that follow, write how often you use each item; then jot a short note to explain whether you are pleased with how you are using (or not using) the item.

- All the time
- Regularly, but intermittently
- Occasionally
- Rarely
- Never

Use the following chart to help you get started with this important step.

Technology	Intended Use	Actual Use
Desktop Computer	Prepare all documents, write all communications when working from home office, connect to Internet, manage electronic files.	Occasionally; end up using my laptop all the time so I don't have to synchronize my data. Use the desktop PC mostly to connect to the Internet, play computer games, shop the Web.
Laptop Computer	Same as desktop computer, above, but use when traveling or working away from the office.	All the time; prefer it to the desktop PC. Also means I don't have to synchronize data on two computers.
Palm/Other Handheld	For scheduling purposes; to jot down notes.	Never; it's a dead weight in the bottom of my briefcase. I find I prefer my old, beat-up paper-based scheduler.

CONTINUED

Technology	Intended Use	Actual Use
Fax machine	Send documents to clients.	Rarely; send most docs via e-mail or using my computer's fax capability, but still feel I need it for the odd document that must be faxed.
B&W laser printer	Print all documents for which I need a paper copy, including e-mails, Web information I want to save.	Regularly, but intermittently; I find I need color copies more often now, so I end up going to Kinko's a lot.
Cell phone	Improve/accelerate availability to client base; also to stay in touch with family and friends.	All the time; but it's starting to drive me crazy; people call me on it for the most trivial reasons.
VCR	To tape my favorite TV shows when I'm out; to watch rental movies.	Never; I have switched to a DVD player. Now I have stacks of videos I never watch and the VCR is collecting dust.
Television	Entertainment, relaxation; stay current on world events.	All the time; but everyone in my household has his or her own and now I feel that TV is keeping us apart. Also, it's difficult to monitor what my kids are watching, and my spouse and I never talk anymore, except during commercials.

You get the idea. It should quickly become clear whether you are making the best use of your technologies. And you should realize that you have choices and opportunities for improvement. The next section explains how to take advantage of those choices and how to "tame the technology" that is not working for you.

Rethinking Your Use of Technology

Everyone has to decide individually what technologies work for them and which do not, and sometimes you have to experiment a little. If you had entries in the preceding exercise that you want to change, think about what you could do—or stop doing—to implement the change.

Using another sheet of paper, jot down ways you might change your use of specific technologies. Here are some ideas to get you started:

> **The desktop computer.** If you prefer to use your laptop for most things, why not consider buying a docking station so you can use your laptop as a desktop model at home?

> **The fax machine and laser printer.** If you still need to fax paper on occasion, you might conclude that it is time to replace your fax machine and laser printer with a multipurpose machine that faxes, scans, copies, and prints originals in color and black and white. This technology could end up saving you space, time, and money.

> **The handheld.** If you are not using it or if you do not like to use it, admit it and move on. Not all technology is for everyone. Everyone works differently.

> **The cell phone.** A cell phone can be a major convenience, but it can also become the bane of your existence. If you are starting to feel trapped by being constantly available, set boundaries. Stop giving the number to everyone. Turn off the cell phone when you are at home, in transit, in a meeting, or when you just need to think—you decide.

These suggestions are just to get you started. Just don't lose sight of the goal for this first part of taming technology: You control the technology; do not let it control you.

If you decide to let go of some technologies, do not just "stash" the outdated, outmoded, unused electronics. Donate these machines to worthy organizations such as schools, places of worship, homeless shelters, hospitals, girls and boys clubs, women's shelters, or return-to-work programs. Doing so will make you feel good—and, in many cases, you can claim the donations as a tax write-off.

Stop Before You Shop

After analyzing the technologies you have, the second part of making better technology choices involves being more cautious in shopping for new products or upgrades. Your goal is to resist the temptation to buy something you do not really need and may rarely or never use.

Before you make a new technology purchase, ask yourself the following questions:

➤ *Do I really need it?* (For example, is it necessary for your work? Will it help your children do their schoolwork more efficiently?)

➤ *Will it make my life easier in some way?* (Will it help you do a better job?)

➤ *Will it enable me to stay in touch more easily with friends and family?* (If you have 15 contact numbers for your family of three, wouldn't you say that is too many?)

➤ *Do I already own something similar that is working well?*

➤ *Will the new item significantly increase my ability to perform my tasks?*

Two Steps to Making a Sound Selection

If you answered yes to one or more of the preceding questions, then you may decide to go ahead with the purchase. Before you do, though, follow these steps:

Step 1: Research carefully before you invest in a new technology

➤ Read product reviews. Many newspapers and magazines have regular columns or reports on the "hottest" new technologies. Many of these reviews are also available online. Television news programs review new tech products too.

➤ Get references. Ideally, these should come from friends or colleagues who have similar work styles as you, are in the same profession, or are similarly tech-savvy. Getting references is especially important to do along with reading product reviews. Keep in mind, the people who write the reviews are more tech-proficient than you are (it is their job, after all) and cannot possibly have the typical-shopper perspective you need to make the best decision for your needs.

Step 2: Comparison shop—online and on land

> ➤ Visit at least three stores that sell the same merchandise.

> ➤ Do not just compare prices. Evaluate the expertise of the sales reps and the quality of customer service. If a sales rep talks down to you or is impatient when explaining the product's functionality, go somewhere else.

> ➤ Ask about trial periods. Some places will allow you to try the product for a period of time, money-back guaranteed if you do not like it or realize you will never use it. Be sure to save your receipts and packaging.

Too Much of a Good Thing?

If you think technology is driving you crazy, consider this poor man, who drove off the road because of technology (from Reuters news service, January 15, 1999):

Dateline: Kiev—A Ukraine businessman who bought a pager for each member of his staff as a New Year's gift was so alarmed when all 50 of them went off at the same time that he drove his car into a lamppost.

The businessman was returning from the pager shop when the accident happened. According to the local daily paper, "With no more than 100 meters to go to the office, the 50 pagers on the back seat suddenly burst out screeching. The businessman was so startled that he simply let go of the steering wheel and the car ploughed into a lamppost."

After he had assessed the damage to the car, the businessman turned his attention to the message on the 50 pagers. They all read the same: "Congratulations on a successful purchase."

Guiding Principles

When evaluating technologies—new and old—apply the following as guiding principles:

➤ Use what works for you. New technologies are not necessarily the best. Proven technologies, ones that you already know how to use, are the best technologies.

➤ Do not forget the simplest, no-fail "technology": Thinking. Turn off the computer, the television, the phone—and think about what you have seen, heard, and read.

PART 7

Coping at Home

Balancing Work and Home Life

Do you eat data for breakfast? Do you reach for your phone to listen to voice mail even before your reach for your spouse/child/dog/coffee? Is your home or home office starting to look like a branch of a "big box" electronics store? At night, do you and the members of your household spend more time in front of separate screens (television, computer, video, etc.) than interacting with one another or with friends? Have you ever neglected to pay a bill because it got buried and forgotten under a pile of catalogs, newspapers, or magazines? Do you feel you never really relax anymore? Have you forgotten the last time you awoke feeling really rested?

If you answered yes to any—or all—of these questions, you are not alone. Perhaps nowhere are the effects of information anxiety being felt more acutely than at home, where people used to spend their time off enjoying some well-earned "R&R." Today, with technology—thus, information—invading the home as much as everywhere else, people are finding it more difficult to separate their "outside" lives from their "inside" lives.

Before constant connectivity, clear lines were drawn between home and office or school, between personal and professional: 9 to 5 was the standard time frame and 24/7 was just some weird fraction. At the end of the business and school day, adults and children went home to relax and spend time with those closest to them. Sure, kids always had homework to do, and parents sometimes took work home, but the distinction was clear.

No more. Today, to many stressed-out, information-anxious adults and young-sters alike, 24/7 is the universal time zone, complete with round-the clock avail-ability of people, products, and services. Sometimes it seems the only things unavailable these days are leisure time and a stress-free environment.

This part is about reclaiming the time and place for those activities that are essential to your well-being—your health, your psyche, your relationships—in short, your life!

Making a Wish List

As has been the case throughout this book, the first part of this section involves identifying how the overflow of information has affected you—this time specifically as it relates to your home life, your downtime.

Because home is where you are supposed to be able to let your imagination run wild and indulge in your dreams, this exercise asks you to make a wish list, a quality-of-life improvement list. Indulge your heart's desires. You have nothing to lose—except your information anxiety. Initially, do not edit your list or worry about feasibility or process. Those decisions come later.

I wish...

- ❏ I could get my family to eat dinner together most evenings—and not in front of the television.

- ❏ I had the time (or energy or desire) to go out with friends (or take a class or exercise) at least once a week.

- ❏ I could just throw out all the old newspapers and magazines lying around and turn off the news without worrying I was missing something important.

- ❏ I (and/or my family) could reduce my (our, their) reliance on television (Internet, video games, etc.) for entertainment, and instead spend more time _____ (reading, talking, exercising).

- ❏ I had enough free time to take a bubble bath before dinner every night.

- ❏ Once a week, I could indulge in a technology-free evening (no TV, no Internet, no phone).

- ❏ I could take a "real" vacation (even a short one) during which I didn't stay in touch with my office/clients/colleagues.

- ❏ _____

- ❏ _____

- ❏ _____

- ❏ _____

Making Your Wishes Come True

Review your wish list. No doubt your wishes mirror many of the causes of information anxiety that have been discussed throughout this book:

- ➤ Too much input from too many sources

- ➤ Paper pile-ups

- ➤ Technological infestation

- ➤ Constant connectivity

- ➤ No free or unscheduled time

- ➤ Too many distractions

But that also means you already have the knowledge (remember the difference between knowledge and information?) to make your wishes come true—that is, to implement the strategies you have learned to lighten your information overload and quiet your information anxiety.

You have read about techniques for managing information and technology. How many of them have you actually tried? The exercise on the next page, in the form of a pop quiz, makes a helpful reminder of actions you could and should be taking now, today, to get real relief for your information anxiety at home.

HOW DO YOU SPELL RELIEF?

How many of the following ways are you using to regain control over your life? For each question, assign one of these values:

> 10 points if you have fully implemented the strategy
> 5 points if you have started, but need to do more, more regularly
> 1 point if all you have done is think about the task

1. Have you cancelled subscriptions to magazines and newspapers you do not really read? _____

2. Have you called credit card companies to stop the inflow of pre-approved credit card offers? _____

3. Two-part question: Have you established paper-dumping criteria? _____ If yes, have you implemented the paper-dumping process—that is, have you reduced your paper pile-ups? _____

4. Have you disposed of (properly, of course) outdated or nonworking technologies that are taking up space in your home or home office? _____

5. Have you implemented an electronic filing system for your e-mail? _____ For your word processing documents? _____

6. Have you set up a paper filing system, one that ensures that you can, at a moment's notice, put your hands on any documents that are important to the business of your life—bills, medical records, tax records? _____

7. Have you scheduled quiet time for yourself every day, to just think, meditate, or relax? _____

8. Have you started your "data diet," as discussed in Part 3? Do you, for example, give yourself one night off a week from the news? _____

9. Have you cut back on multi-tasking? Do you, for example, really listen to your friends when they call rather than listening with one ear to your friend and the other to the evening news? _____

10. Have you defined what "quality information" is for you so that you can more easily and quickly filter that which you do not need? _____

Fair Game

If you have implemented different strategies from those covered in the quiz, be sure to give yourself credit for them. This quiz is intended only to remind you of the many ways it is possible to regain control over your life quickly and easily using better information management techniques. It is not meant to make you feel more stressed because you have not done them all.

Scoring:

90-120: Congratulations! You are becoming a top-flight information manager.

75-89: Keep up the good work. Chances are, your information anxiety is noticeably less intense.

60-74: Hmmm. You've made a start but really need to make more of an effort.

0-59: C'mon, you do realize, don't you, that only you can manage the information in your life?

Taking Action on Your Newfound Knowledge

A strategy is only as good as its implementation. At home, generally four things stall people in these efforts:

> **Bad habits**

> **Procrastination**

> **Lack of time**

> **Lack of knowledge**

Habits, as everyone knows, are hard to break; and procrastination is equally challenging to overcome, especially at home, when you are exhausted and just want to flop on the couch. So the guideline here is *easy does it!*

The surefire path to failure is to try to change everything at once. At the end of another too-long day when you arrive home to find yet another pile of junk mail and catalogs in your mailbox, unpaid bills on the kitchen counter, and everyone else in your household glued to television or computer screens, resist the urge to create a whirlwind of change prompted by frustration. It will never stick. Instead, take these two steps:

> Sit down at the table with your wish list, next month's (ideally mostly blank) calendar, and a pen

> Schedule two information- or technology-reducing activities per week: one that qualifies as a wish fulfillment (i.e., fun or relaxing) and the other that qualifies more as a chore (i.e., not really fun or relaxing, but that will give you more time for both)

The sample calendar below includes some of the items from the wish list presented earlier to give you an idea of how to get started.

Mon	Tue	Wed	Thur	Fri	Sat	Sun
	1 Dinner at the table; TV and other "noise" turned off	2	3	4	5 Sort through paper piles; throw out outdated publications, catalogs	6
7 Tech-free night: no TV, computers, etc.; instead, read, talk, play board games	8	9	10 Call local organizations to arrange donation of outdated, unused electronics.	11	12	13
14	15 Pay this month's bills; file receipts.	16	17	18	19 Begin one-day news "fast."	20
21	22	23	24 Take long, luxuriant bubble bath after dinner.	25 Call two credit card companies to request removal from mailing lists.	26	27
28	29 Exercise: take 30-min. walk after dinner	30	31	1	2	3 Set up spam filters on e-mail program.

If even that is too much for you because you already have a lot scheduled for next month, just do one a week, but alternate between the fun or relaxing strategies and the more chore-like ones. Do not forget that once you set up spam filters on your e-mail program, for example, you won't have to do that weekly. You will quickly work through your chores, and the time you had dedicated to those can be filled with more interesting, fun activities.

Tip

Post your info-management calendar where you will see it. Be sure not to add it to any paper pile you have been building!

Committing to Change

This step has only one requirement and does not involve lists or exercises; nevertheless, you may find it the most difficult to achieve:

Do not give up.

What if you accomplished only one of the scheduled items on your calendar—and it wasn't even a "fun one"? Maybe you managed to haul out months-old piles of newspapers, magazines, and catalogs, but that is it. You did nothing else all month to relieve the information overload at home.

Do not feel defeated. Instead, focus on how good it felt to take that step toward control. Didn't that single act make you feel free? The world did not come to an end because you didn't go through every magazine or newspaper you had been saving "just in case" it had something you wanted to read. And certainly your bank balance looks better for not indulging in a catalog-induced shopping spree.

Now be encouraged to do more. As you read this, why not commit, maybe, to a mini-vacation during which you communicate only with your thoughts (or your best friend or significant other, if you prefer to take someone with you—just make sure your companion agrees to "disconnect" too). Take your cell phone along if you must, in case of legitimate emergencies, but commit to the following:

> ➤ I will not check my voice mail

> ➤ I will not check my e-mail

> ➤ I will not call my office or my clients

> ➤ I will not check the stock market

> ➤ I will not read or listen to the news

> ➤ I will not check sports results

Feel scary? Try it; you'll like it.

You Call This Getting Away?

Think back to your last vacation. Did you really get away? Or did you check your voice mail the minute your plane landed at your destination? Did you take a laptop with you even though it meant you had to take out your favorite pair of walking shoes to make room for it in the suitcase? Did you take your cell phone with you while touring the French countryside because you wanted to be sure your manager or clients could reach you at all times? Did you forget your sunglasses but remember your pager as you set off to stroll the beach in the Bahamas?

Sadly, alarmingly, this is the way many people "vacation" these days. Their bodies may go to a different location, but their minds stay fully connected to work. In fact, according to a survey conducted for *American Demographics* magazine by the New Brunswick, New Jersey-based NFO Plog Research (the travel and leisure division of NFO WorldGroup), the majority of Americans are expected to stay in touch with the office. More surprising, perhaps, is that most of those surveyed did not object.

Of the full-time working adults surveyed online by *American Demographics* in May 2002:

➤ 69% said that they would prefer to keep their office contact to a minimum while on vacation, but expected–and accepted–to be interrupted by circumstances requiring their attention

➤ 8% (nearly 1 in 10) said they expected to communicate regularly with the office while away

➤ 3% take the initiative and check in with the office

➤ 46% check their e-mail

Finally, two-thirds of working Americans (68%) take at least one electronic communication device with them on vacation.

When Home and Office Collide

The information revolution expanded the concept of the workplace. The office could no longer be defined as the place to which people with full-time jobs went every day, often dressed uniformly, to work "for somebody" according to preset schedules. Widespread technological advances of the past 25 years have turned the office into an economic frontier, which quickly has come to be explored and settled by professionals from all walks of business life.

Redefining the Home Office

Gone are the days when working at home meant "homemaker" or someone sitting at the kitchen table stuffing envelopes. Gone too are the days when home office meant the headquarters of some corporate giant. Now home office can refer to a refashioned garage in a suburban house, a cordoned-off corner of a small apartment, a spare bedroom rewired for sound and videoconferencing, or a laundry room now doing double-duty.

Today, the *office* is anything but one-size-fits-all, for the term must accommodate:

➤ The SOHO (small office/home office) entrepreneur, running his own business (often Web-based), selling products or services to a consumer base that extends, potentially, all over the world

➤ The independent contractor or freelancer, working frequently on-site at a client's office, and using her home office as coordination space, for filing, managing accounts, and keeping up with correspondence

➤ The telecommuter, who is still working full-time for a corporate employer and stays connected via various technologies, only rarely meeting face-to-face with co-workers

➤ The mobile businessperson, who sets up workspace in conference rooms, airline terminals, hotel rooms—wherever the work has to be done—using his home office as a refueling station, to replenish supplies, follow up on the last trip, and arrange the next

➤ The full-time employee with an office in a traditional work environment who has arranged a flexible work schedule that includes two to three days a week working from home

➤ A combination of one or more of the above, and many others besides

The Challenges of Working from Home

This workplace expansion has come at a price. As both corporate and entrepreneurial types have embraced the innumerable possibilities of the redefined home office, a new set of challenges has emerged.

Anyone who works at home—whether full, part, or extra time—has begun to suffer from a particularly acute form of information overload. Its primary symptom is the blurring of the line between personal and professional life.

People who work from home often fall into the habit of "giving away" their time to the job and the home:

➤ To clients or colleagues who think that because you work from home it is okay to call at all hours

➤ To friends or family who do not respect that you are hard at work even if your office is next door to the bedroom or the washing machine

➤ To neighbors who know you are at home and think nothing of dropping by for a visit or to ask a favor

Setting Boundaries Between Home and Office

For home-office workers, the two most important aspects of information management are:

> **Drawing boundaries between home and office**

> **Honoring those boundaries**

This section presents six guidelines for helping you set—and keep—boundaries between your home and your home office.

> **Use the right space.** Consider carefully the space in your home that you use as your office. This may be difficult to do if, for example, you live in a small house or apartment, but lots of tools and modular furniture options are available today that make it possible to clearly and cleanly separate the work area from the home.

> **Install the right equipment.** Research carefully the technologies that will help you increase your productivity yet not overwhelm you.

> **Set a schedule.** The advantage of working from home is that, often, you can set your own hours. The disadvantage is that if you do not clearly define those hours, you may never get anything done. Once you have set the schedule, make it known so that everyone understands when you are working.

> **Stick to your schedule.** Know when to stop working. When your office is just steps down the hall, it is tempting to put in just a little more time or make a few more calls. Do not do it. Close the door, draw the curtain or divider, turn off the computer, and "go home."

> **Learn to say no.** Learn to say it to clients or colleagues when they call "after hours." Ideally, you should have a separate phone line for work, and if so, do not pick up the phone in your off hours. Learn to say no to friends and family when you are working. You cannot afford to be less professional than your corporate counterparts while you are at work, nor can you afford to jeopardize your personal relationships by letting work interfere with them.

➤ **Minimize multi-tasking.** People fall prey to the multi-tasking demon at home perhaps more than anywhere else, especially if they work from home. Remember, multi-tasking makes you less—not more—efficient.

Tip ══

Today, millions of people work from home offices, and information is widely available to help them succeed. A good resource is the Small Business Administration (www.sba.org). Or simply take a Web tour of the myriad home-office sites now online. (Just be sure to filter your search criteria based on your needs or you will be overwhelmed by the number of "hits" you receive.) A good place to start is Working Solo (www.workingsolo.com), whose founder, Terri Lonier, has written several books especially for the small office/home office (SOHO) market.

Keeping the Home Court Advantage

Do you believe you can make your wishes come true for ensuring that your personal life is not overburdened by today's—and tomorrow's—technologies and the information that comes with them? You can, you know.

By implementing the information- and technology-management strategies described in this section and throughout the book, you will quickly begin to see a significant drop in your information anxiety.

SUMMARY

Quick-Step Review

This book may seem to present something of an irony in that it asks you to assimilate more information to lighten your information overload. But there is a good reason. As explained in Part 1, more new information has been produced in the last 30 years than in the last 5,000, and most of it has been the result of even faster-developing technologies. And we humans have been expected to cope with all of that while on the run—almost literally.

It is no surprise then that many of us are out of breath, falling behind, and, in some cases, close to giving up. This book has demonstrated that you can slow down, catch your breath, and still survive life in the fast lane—but it does require you to backtrack a little, to figure out how and why you are suffering from information anxiety. Only then can you move forward effectively and efficiently and still have time for the important things in your life.

Change, however much you may want to implement it, does not happen over-night, so do not add stress to your life by expecting to be able to put to use right away all the strategies and techniques described. Focus on those you know will make the greatest difference in your life the most quickly, and start there. Once you have learned to manage information in one area, move on to the next.

The purpose of this quick-step review of the information-management topics covered in this book is to enable you to refresh your memory, at a glance, about all you have learned.

Part 1: Information Anxiety

You have heard it said that recognizing a problem is the first step toward solving it. We began by discussing how the "experts" define information anxiety and the effects it has on many people. But because everyone is different, this part asked you to:

> ➤ Figure out how you are currently handling the onslaught of information in your life.

> ➤ Identify ways to find relief, by acknowledging your strengths and weaknesses for dealing with the information you handle every day.

> ➤ Make a list of information anxiety relief goals.

> ➤ Set priorities among your goals.

Part 2: Multi-Tasking

Multi-tasking, it turns out, is highly overrated as a means of coping with information overload and anxiety. In fact, it has been scientifically proven not to work. To help you calculate the price you are paying for using multi-tasking as a coping mechanism, this part asked you to:

➤ Determine if you are getting the results you like or need when you multi-task.

➤ Find your way out of the multi-tasking maze by: (a) learning to estimate task times accurately, (b) making to-do lists rather than expecting your brain to remember everything, and (c) limiting interruptions and concentrating.

➤ Multi-task smart when you do have to multi-task—that means using common sense, monitoring your progress, and being honest with yourself.

➤ Give yourself credit for all you do accomplish everyday. Count what is done, not what you did not do.

Part 3: Filtering Information

This part explained that most people today know how to gather data but not how to convert it into useable information. This is a vital distinction for managing information. Recall that 80% of the information most people keep they never refer to again.

To separate the informational wheat from the chaff, this part asked you to:

➤ Compare the amount of time you tap into various sources of information every day (TV, the Internet, e-mail, telephones, print media, etc.) vs. the time you give yourself to review, think about, and evaluate all that information—that is, to convert data into knowledge.

➤ Define for yourself what quality information is. Does it help you do your job better or take better care of your home and family?

➤ Reduce the amount of time you spend gathering information (e.g., turn off the TV, unplug the phone after a certain hour, etc.).

➤ Use electronic information filters. This includes installing–and using–e-mail filters, experimenting with search engines to find the one(s) that give you quality information as you define it.

➤ Sort and store the information you do need and want so that you can access it at a moment's notice.

Part 4: Managing Messaging Systems

E-mail and voice mail: Where would we be without them? We depend on them for so much. But they are also major sources of information overload and its attendant stress. Too often, it seems they run us, not the other way around.

To return control to where it belongs–to you–this part asked you to:

➤ Pinpoint the processes you use today to handle your e-mail and voice mail messages.

➤ Identify the points of failure in those processes (e.g., you let messages interrupt your thoughts and your work by accepting them upon arrival).

➤ Calculate how much time it really takes to read or listen and respond to messages.

➤ Restructure the processes. For e-mail, this means taking the time to learn all the options your e-mail program has for managing messages (file options, filtering aids, spam control, and more). For voice mail, this means learning how to give and take messages effectively and efficiently.

➤ Schedule (to limit) how often and when to check e-mail and voice mail. This will depend on your occupation, of course, but a good rule of thumb is at the beginning and end of each workday, and perhaps a third check-in around midday.

Part 5: Processing Paper

Advances in technology brought us more paper, not less. And paper—in the form of memos, faxes, reports, newspapers and magazines, downloaded Web content, and more—is perhaps the most visible sign of information overload. It is probably tripping you up daily.

To help you get out from under all that paper, this part asked you to:

> ➤ Watch how you allow paper pile-ups to begin (e.g., you push a memo aside because you do not know how to respond, or do not have the time; then it gets lost in the shuffle).

> ➤ Admit what is stopping you from attacking the piles: fear of dumping? resistance to filing? lack of time?

> ➤ Act! Dispose of disposable incoming mail (e.g., junk mail and subscriptions to magazines you never read).

> ➤ Use your imagination to find innovative ways of reducing the paper in your life.

> ➤ In the face of paper, ask these four simple questions: What is the worst thing that would happen if I tossed this? Where should I keep it? How long do I need to keep it? How can I remember where to find it?

Part 6: Taming Technology

The image of technology as a beast that needs taming before it overpowers you has become prevalent in the media. The purpose of this part was to help you domesticate the unruly beast.

To do so, it asked you to:

> ➤ Know what you have. This involves, first, itemizing the technologies you own; second, estimating how often and how well you use those technologies; and, third, taming the technologies by getting rid of some of them, consolidating others, or changing how you use still others.

➤ Stop before you shop. Simply, consider carefully any new piece of equipment or electronic gadget you are thinking of buying. It is too easy to get "sold" by advertising and marketing campaigns, or to feel compelled to "keep up with the Joneses." Always ask yourself: Do I really need it? If the answer is yes, do your homework: Get references and comparison shop.

Part 7: Coping at Home

For most people, long gone are the days when home was the haven from the outside world of work, school, and stress. Now the lines between "inside" and "outside" are so blurred that they are almost invisible. But you need leisure time and a stress-free environment.

To help you redraw that important boundary between personal and professional, this part asked you to:

➤ Make a wish list of quality-of-life improvements you would like to make.

➤ Review your list in the context of the information-management issues raised throughout this book to determine which of those issues are interfering with your personal life the most dramatically.

➤ Review the information-management strategies you have implemented so far. If you are still in the thinking-about-it stage, it is time to take action.

➤ Start slow and easy. A good way is to schedule on your calendar one or two wish-list items per week.

➤ Commit to change. No matter how much old habits or procrastination impede your progress, give yourself points for trying, then try again. And again.

That last guideline—commit to change—is perhaps the most important of the entire book. Most change is an evolutionary process, one whose individual steps cannot always be seen on a daily basis, which may cause you to become discouraged. But when you commit to improving the quality of your life, the changes over time will be obvious and often dramatic—and more than worth the effort.

Good luck to you. You will succeed.

[1] Richard Saul Wurman, *Information Anxiety* (New York: Doubleday, 1989).

[2] Peter Large, *The Micro Revolution Revisited* (Rowman & Littlefield, 1984).

[3] International Data Corporation.

[4] Karl Albrecht, "Info Overload," *Training & Development* (February 2001).

[5] *Office Systems: The Magazine for Small and Medium Offices* (March 1997)

[6] David Shenk, *Data Smog: Surviving the Information Glut* (HarperSanFrancisco, 1997).

Recommended Reading

Brod, Craig. *Technostress: The Human Cost of the Computer Revolution*. Reading, MA: Addison-Wesley, 1984.

Ellwood, Mark. *Cut the Glut of E-mail*. Toronto: Pace Productivity, Inc., 2002.

Flynn, Nancy, and Tom Flynn. *Writing Effective E-mail: Improving Your Electronic Communication, Revised*. Boston, MA: Thomson Learning, 2003.

Lehmkuhl, Dorothy, and Dolores Cotter Lamping. *Organizing for the Creative Person: Right-Brain Styles for Conquering Clutter, Mastering Time, and Reaching Your Goals*. New York: Crown Publishers, 1993.

Lively, Lynn. *Managing Information Overload*. New York: AMACOM, 1996.

Morgenstern, Julie. *Organizing from the Inside Out: The Foolproof System for Organizing Your Home, Your Office, and Your Life*. New York: Henry Holt and Company, 1998.

Ohler, Jason. *Taming the Beast: Choice and Control in the Electronic Jungle.*. Bloomington, IN: Technos Press, 1999.

Pollar, Odette. *365 Ways to Simplify Your Work Life*. Chicago: Dearborn Trade, 1996.

Pollar, Odette. *Organizing Your Work Space*. Boston, MA: Thomson Learning, 1999.

Pollar, Odette. *Simplify Your Life: A Step-by-Step Guide to Better Living*. New York: MJF Books, 1999.

Shenk, David. *Data Smog: Surviving the Information Glut*. New York: HarperCollins, 1997.

Vetter, Greg. *Find It in Five Seconds: Gaining Control in the Information Age*. Seattle: Hara Publishing, 1999.

Wurman, Richard Saul. *Information Anxiety: What to Do When Information Doesn't Tell You What You Need to Know*. New York: Doubleday, 1989.

For More Information

The National Association of Professional Organizers
35 Technology Parkway South, Suite 150
Norcross, GA 30092
Phone: 770-325-3440
Fax: 770-263-8825
www.napo.net

Information Stress Management Association
Attn: James C. Quick, Ph.D.
University of Texas at Arlington
Box 19467
Arlington, TX 76019-0467
www.stress-management-isma.org

Your Feedback Is Important!

This book is the result of feedback from many clients and from hundreds of people in training workshops and seminars. Your reactions to this book are important. Please help by providing your feedback.

What information management strategies have you found to be most useful?

_____

_____

What was helpful about this book?

_____

_____

Where can you see areas for improvement?

_____

_____

Any additional comments?

_____

_____

Thank you for taking the time to respond. Please mail, fax, or e-mail this form to:

Odette Pollar
Smart Ways to Work
1441 Franklin St., Suite 301
Oakland, CA 94612
Phone: 800-599-TIME
Fax: 510-763-0790
E-mail: odette@smartwaystowork.com

NOTES

Now Available From

Books•Videos•CD-ROMs•Computer-Based Training Products

Subject Areas Include:

Management
Human Resources
Communication Skills
Personal Development
Sales/Marketing
Finance
Coaching and Mentoring
Customer Service/Quality
Small Business and Entrepreneurship
Training
Life Planning
Writing

Surviving Information Overload